THE REAL PROFIT DRIVERS: MANAGING THE CPVs

Dr. Albert D. Bates
Profit Planning Group

D. M. KREG PUBLISHING

The Real Profit Drivers: Managing the CPVs

ISBN: 978-0-9893578-3-8

Cover Design: The Cover Counts, thecovercounts@gmail.com

Interior Layout and Design: Ronda Taylor, www.taylorbydesign.com

▪ Contents

■ Dedication

To Dr. Jay Smith, the man who made the University of Industrial Distribution happen.

■ Acknowledgements

This book is based upon the collective research efforts of the Profit Planning Group over the course of the last twenty years. It is not possible to thank everybody who provided inspiration and encouragement or corrected my thought process. However, I would be remiss if I did not specifically thank three groups.

Mentors: Dr. Bert C. McCammon who started me in financial research, Dr. Alton Doody who demonstrated that you should try to climb every mountain even if you know it can't be climbed and Dan Riley who gave our struggling company a chance when nobody else would.

Associates: Jamie Adams who made my prose as close to comprehensible as is possible, Letitia Marti who put up with my bizarre ideas and Dr. Bill McCleave who served as an outstanding first reader.

Inspiration: In a way that nobody will ever understand, I have been inspired by Ed Lewis, Joan Westin and Eddie Feigner. Real road warriors all.

■ Report Highlights

Much of what is "known" about profitability in distribution is just plain wrong. Urban legend and clever anecdotes dominate too much of management's thinking about profitability.

This report identifies what actually drives profit. It does so by examining the financial performance on the Critical Profit Variables (CPVs) of 885 distributors in 17 different lines of trade. It is the largest study of profitability ever undertaken in distribution.

Some of the key findings which should be noted include:

- Firms that are able to control gross margin and operating expenses in tandem are by far the most profitable. Firms that focus on any other combination of the CPVs are demonstrably less profitable.
- Larger firms in a single line of trade are more profitable than smaller firms. There is a strong penalty for being even slightly smaller than the typical firm, in any distribution industry.
- Sales growth leads to higher profits, but only if the firm can significantly outpace its peers in terms of sales growth. Growing slightly faster than the industry has no real impact on profitability.
- Gross margin has a dramatic impact on profitability as long as the firm does not have to over-invest in inventory (through advanced buying) to generate the high margin.
- Operating expense control, especially with regard to payroll, represents the single most important driver of profitability. Nothing else even comes close.
- Both the Days Sales Outstanding (DSO) and inventory turnover have only a modest impact on profit.
- The majority of firms emphasize actions that do not improve profitability. Only a small percentage of firms are able to combine the CPVs in a way that benefits financial results.
- In order to make improvements, firms need to have access to a strong set of financial and operating metrics that provide comparisons to their peers.

■ Introduction

This report has only one purpose. That is to identify the factors that really drive profit in distribution. It examines six different Critical Profit Variables (CPVs), including sales volume, sales growth, the gross margin percentage, the operating expense percentage, the days sales outstanding (DSO) and inventory turnover.

The analytical process is entirely empirical. That is, the report will examine the profit performance of a large sample of distribution firms to see how changes in sales, gross margin and the like actually impact profit. It will focus on the statistical linkage between the CPVs and profit.

For each of the CPVs, two issues will be addressed. The first is the importance of the CPV. Is controlling the CPV absolutely essential to increasing profit or can it be given benign neglect? The goal is to establish a priority ranking for the CPVs as a guideline for management.

The second issue is to determine how strong the firm's performance on each of the CPVs has to be to impact profit significantly. There may be some variables that require performance in the top 25% of all firms. There may be others where just being near the industry norm is good enough. Knowing which variable falls in which group is essential for success.

It must be emphasized again that the analysis in this report is based upon the actual financial performance generated by a large sample of firms. Every distribution consultant—whether in sales training, inventory control, pricing or any other topic—has an idea about what is important. Too often those beliefs are based on anecdotal evidence. This report replaces anecdotes with empirical information.

The findings will offer some surprises for many executives. Such surprises should lead to improved profit performance.

■ Section One:
The Search for Profitability Relationships

One of the most widely debated financial aspects of distribution management is in identifying what the firm should emphasize in its profit-improvement activities. As an illustration, should the firm emphasize driving additional sales volume to spread overhead expenses across a larger base? Conversely, should it try to enhance its gross margin percentage even if that action diminishes the rate of sales growth? From a completely different perspective, should the firm focus on the investment side of the business to reduce its inventory and accounts receivable?

The answer to the "what to work on most aggressively" question depends in large part on the profit impact that different actions have. If sales growth is more productive than gross margin, then sales growth should be emphasized even at the expense of some margin. Before taking such action, though, it is imperative to be sure that increasing sales really is more important than improving gross margin. Too often "what to work on" is driven by management preference, historical accident, or recently-recited consulting advice rather than fact. Ultimately, real-world information is required to meet the what-to-work-on challenge.

As long as all of the firms in an industry are somewhat similar in terms of their financial structure (similar sales levels, similar gross margin percentages, etc.) the issue is relatively straightforward. The task is to simply find the most successful firms and emulate their actions.

The problem in many instances, though, is that some successful firms do one thing (emphasize sales growth) while others do something that is entirely the opposite (focus on gross margin). There are usually similarities among the most-successful firms, but never complete uniformity of direction.

In distribution, the issue of developing global suggestions as to where to focus the firm's efforts is complicated by the fact that different lines of trade within the broad distribution umbrella have dramatically different economics. Can the successful actions of a firm in a low-gross margin sector of distribution really be applied to a high-gross margin sector? Even within a single line of trade there are sharp variations in operating economics, reflecting different pockets of opportunity.

Despite these challenges, there is a strong desire among managers to identify the "keys to profitability" that can be applied universally in distribution. The author has received numerous requests to compare profit results across different lines of trade. This report is an effort to provide some conclusions about what drives profitability. While there is no "sliver bullet" that automatically improves profitability, there are some sets of actions that *dramatically* increase the likelihood of success.

Identifying Appropriate Actions

The task of identifying specific actions to improve performance can be approached in three very different ways. First, from an observational approach, it is possible to see how firms focus their time and effort. If firms spend a lot of time and energy on sales training, then clearly that is considered an essential vehicle for profit improvement.

Second, financial modeling can provide insights into what *should* drive profit to higher levels. This involves using programs such as Excel® to map the relationship between the CPVs and profitability. Such models provide the ability to change a CPV (such as sales) and follow the impact on the financial results of the firm. This "what if" form of analysis is widely used by profitability analysts.

Finally, with an adequate sample, empirical analysis can be used to measure statistically how different actions drive profit. This is the approach that is employed here. Before reviewing the results it is important to understand the conclusions that can be drawn from the first two approaches. The issue at hand is to compare what management is focused on with the factors that the empirical analysis says should be emphasized.

Observation

It is possible to take a "wisdom of the crowd" approach to see where management thinks the greatest payoff is to be found. From this perspective, the overwhelming answer is that sales is the profit driver given most credence.

At almost any convention, the sessions on increasing sales are the big-attendance events. When pure sales training/motivation sessions are combined with ancillary sales topics—economic forecasting, developing new marketing strategies, driving additional sales via the internet—it seems that at least two-thirds of management's interest and enthusiasm is geared towards increasing sales volume.

As another example, the University of Industrial Distribution is one of the premier training programs for distributors. In 2014, a total of 17 out of 33 sessions were devoted to some aspect of increasing sales. It is a message that management wants to hear and likes to hear repeatedly.

The preceding two paragraphs may seem like nothing more than random anecdotes dropped into the discussion. Actually, these points are extremely important. An overly-heavy emphasis on sales could ultimately prove dysfunctional. This point will be discussed at length later in this report.

The truth is that popularity does not necessarily correlate with performance improvement. A lot of efforts to increase sales may actually impair profit. Even so, the management team in most organizations is rooting for sales to be the most significant key to profitability. Increasing sales is fun and exciting, regardless of the economic payoff. Analysts argue against sales at their peril.

Financial Modeling

Programs such as Excel provide the basis for building highly-sophisticated models of distributor performance. As a mea culpa the author must confess to having spent the last twenty years developing such models in a wide range of industries both inside and outside of distribution.[1] Such models have proven to be extremely powerful tools in channeling the efforts of individual firms toward improving financial results.

Modeling inevitably produces the conclusion that three factors are the keys to profitability. The most important of the factors is gross margin, even if the margin dollars come at the expense of sales. The second factor is expense control. Finally, sales is a contributing factor, but is mired in third place. Interestingly, inventory and accounts receivable reductions seldom have a significant impact on profitability in such models.

Modeling has the serious limitation of assuming that as one CPV—such as gross margin—is changed, the other CPVs change in a highly-predictable manner. In the daily operation of distribution businesses, such precise interaction between variables seldom exists.

Modeling is ideal for examining "what could be done" to improve performance. It simply does not have the ability to address what is actually being done. That is, it can't determine if high-gross margin firms—in aggregate—perform better or worse than low-gross margin ones. It is equally limited in analyzing any other profitability driver.

The limitations associated with both observational analysis and financial modeling suggest a need to identify the underlying factors that really cause some firms to perform better or worse financially than their peers. This can only be accomplished via some form of empirical analysis, which is the focus of this report.

---

1   The conclusions of such modeling can be seen in Dr. Albert D. Bates, *Breaking Down the Profit Barriers in Distribution*, D. M. Kreg Publishing, 2014.

Empirical Analysis

By far the most powerful approach for measuring the impact of management decisions on profitability is to examine the diverse actions of a lot of companies and see how said actions actually influence profitability. While this is the most powerful, it also is inordinately expensive and time consuming. However, the results may well be worth the effort if some generalizations can be developed that apply to a wide range of companies under a broad range of conditions.

One of the most recent empirical research efforts in distribution is the work of the Deloitte distribution research team. They analyzed the performance of a number (unspecified) of publicly-held distribution firms in three different lines of trade. The results of the project have only been released in summary form, but an understanding of the conclusions can be developed.[2]

Essentially, the study suggests that management should have a two-pronged profit plan. The first is to develop a value orientation, which appears to be a proxy for gross margin. The second is to generate higher sales volume through a combination of expanded market presence and a close proximity to customers. Both of these actions—enhanced margin and sales growth—have the potential to increase expenses. However, the study suggests that the expense challenge is immaterial in generating higher profitability levels in distribution.

In point of fact, the study argues that expense control through the traditional emphasis on improved operations is *not* a driver of profitability. Going beyond that, the report suggests focusing on value and sales to the virtual exclusion of everything else. It is an interesting and valuable study with a provocative set of conclusions.

The challenges with any empirical analysis involve both the size of the sample and the diversity of the firms in that sample. While the Deloitte study is both helpful and interesting, it suffers somewhat in both aspects.

With regard to the sample, only a small percentage of distributors are publicly-held entities. In addition, such companies tend to be clustered in a few industries. Thus the analysis analyzed only three different lines of trade.

There is another issue with using publicly-available information (annual reports and SEC-mandated 10-K reports for public firms). As would be expected, most public firms disclose as little information as possible because competitors will most certainly scour the reports for useful operating details.

The Deloitte study does a good job in stimulating thinking about profit issues. However, it suffers from the inevitable limitations associated with publicly-available information. This is not really a criticism of the study, it is acceptance of a reality.

---

2   *Driving Enterprise Value in Wholesale Distribution*, Deloitte Development LLC, 2014.

Something more extensive is needed. That need is for some sort of empirical approach that features an adequate sample size, a broad number of different lines of trade and a comprehensive set of variables for analysis.

To summarize, observation can identify what factors management really wishes impacted profitability. Financial modeling can identify what factors should impact profitability. Only some sort of large-scale empirical study can identify what actually does impact profitability.

The Current Project:
A Brief, but Essential Note on Methodology

Management is a lot more interested in results than in an arcane discussion of statistical methodology. Consequently, the engrossing presentation of the statistical techniques employed and the challenges associated with empirical analysis has been relegated to the Appendix. This report can be appreciated fully without ever having to review the details of the methodology.

There are, however, some extremely important issues that must be understood in order to utilize the findings of this research project. The remainder of this section should be considered carefully.

Composition of the Sample

This research report reflects the performance of 885 distributors, both public and private. All of the firms provided complete financial results and accompanying operating details to the financial benchmarking projects conducted by the Profit Planning Group. Such studies go by the names PAR® Report or PROFIT® Report in most industries. In short, the results represent firms that provided lots of details on their businesses.

These firms operate in 17 different lines of trade. While the Profit Planning Group has information on substantially more lines of trade, these are the lines for which there is an adequate sample size as well as significant detail on almost every aspect of the operation of the subject firms. The 17 lines of trade include distributors selling into the industrial, construction and consumer markets. In short, it includes a diverse array of distribution firms.

The data presented are for 2013. This is not really a "so what" statement. Financial performance varies based upon economic conditions; 2013 was selected because it can be characterized as a rather typical year. There was neither a recession, nor an economic surge. The analysis reflects the operations of firms in a mature industry, which is what distribution represents.

Profit Drivers and Profit Results

The report revolves around what are commonly called the Critical Profit Variables (sometimes referred to as the Key Profit Indicators or Key Profit Drivers). These are the global factors that virtually everybody intuits to have an impact on profit for good or bad. They can be thought of as the independent variables in the analysis. The Critical Profit Variables (CPVs) used in this report include:

- Sales, both the magnitude of sales revenue and the rate of sales growth
- Gross margin as a percent of sales
- Total expenses as a percent of sales
- Inventory turnover
- Days sales outstanding (DSO) on accounts receivable

Financial results—or the dependent variables—are measured using two common ratios: Profit Before Taxes (PBT) and Return on Assets (ROA). While these measures really are common, they are frequently measured in very different ways.

PBT in this report is profit before income taxes expressed as a percent of net sales. ROA is that same pre-tax profit number expressed as a percent of the total assets invested in the firm. In both cases profit is measured before income taxes because of the wide variation in tax rates as a result of the firm's type of organization (S corp versus C corp, etc.) and geographic location of the firm (high-tax states versus zero or low-tax ones).

It is essential to note that profit is measured after all expenses. Many such analyses, especially those conducted in academic institutions, tend to use earnings (profit) before interest, taxes, depreciation and amortization. That is, they use EBITDA as a measure of the profitability of base operations.

However, utilizing EBITDA assumes that neither interest nor depreciation are expenses that should be considered in evaluating corporate performance. The reality is that many management actions directly influence both interest and depreciation.

EBITDA is often valuable in evaluating mergers and acquisitions, particularly those where there is the potential to defer capital investments for an extended period of time and where interest expense can be lowered. However, EBITDA distorts results in reviewing the long-term performance of distributors. Therefore, it is not the measure of choice in this analysis.

PBT and ROA are both useful ratios. PBT is the ratio that most managers track consistently because they are reviewing income statements. For some managers, it is virtually the only financial ratio they will encounter as they are not involved in investment decisions. ROA is actually a much more important ratio as it relates profit to investment. Results for both ratios will be presented. It should always be remembered that ROA is the most critical for long-term success.

PBT and ROA are highly correlated. That is, firms with a high ROA inevitably have a high PBT as well. However, the correlation is not perfect. Some actions that help reduce investment levels, such as lowering the DSO, impact ROA much more than PBT. As noted, both measures are employed in this research effort.

Relative Measures

This is the most critical, and thankfully last, portion of the discussion on methodology. The fundamental analytical challenge is that trying to compare results across different lines of trade in distribution involves an inordinately high degree of difficulty. Different lines of trade are, by definition, different. In fact, they are very different.

As an obvious example, it is not feasible to measure the impact of gross margin on PBT or ROA directly. If the sample includes firms in a low-gross margin line of trade (say a gross margin of 10.0% of sales) and firms in a high-gross margin line of trade (say 30.0%), massive distortions are inevitable. In doing the analysis all of the firms from one line of trade will be in the high-margin category while all of the firms in the other line of trade will be in the low-margin category.

Quite simply, such an analysis is meaningless. It does not measure the impact of gross margin. Instead, it measures the result of being in a specific line of trade. A different approach is needed if the real impact of gross margin is to be determined.

In this report, the CPVs are not analyzed on an absolute basis, but are analyzed *relative* to their peers in the *same line of trade*. For example, a firm with an 11.0% gross margin in an industry where the norm is 10.0% is doing 10.0% better than the typical firm. At the same time, a firm with a 22.0% gross margin in an industry with a 20.0% norm is also doing 10.0% better.

Both firms have established a superior gross margin position. The impact of such superior margin performance on profit can be measured directly. Such relative measures are in no way perfect, but do provide some important insights.

As a reminder, readers with an analytical bent can review the details of the methodology in the Appendix. That discussion includes both the advantages and problems associated with the relative measure methodology.

The primary method of analysis in this report is to break the results on each CPV (using relative figures in all instances) into quintiles. That is, the results are broken into five relatively equal-sized groups, each containing about 20.0% of the firms (approximately 177 firms in each group). For each CPV (such as the gross margin percentage) the sample firms are assigned to one of the following categories:

- Far Below Typical
- Slightly Below Typical
- Mid-Range—Near Typical
- Slightly Above Typical
- Far Above Typical

For each group the relative deviation from the typical PBT and ROA figures for the line of trade is reported. For instance, if firms in the fifth quintile enjoy an ROA that is 30.0% higher than is typical in their industry, the figure of 30.0% would be reported for ROA for that group. This is not the actual ROA generated, but *the deviation from the industry norm* for ROA.

A quick example might help. Start with a sector of distribution where the typical gross margin percentage is 20.0% and the typical ROA in the sector is 8.0%. Suppose the fifth quintile on gross margin includes firms with a gross margin that is 30.0% higher than typical. That means this group includes firms whose gross margin is at least 26.0% (20.0% x 1.3 = 30.0% higher).

Also assume that the relative ROA factor for this group is 15.0%. That means that this group coalesces around an ROA of 9.2% (8.0% x 1.15). That would reflect the impact on overall performance associated with doing a superior job with regard to gross margin by itself.

There are 17 different lines of trade included in this research project. Some are high-margin, high-expense lines of trade. Others are low-margin, low-expense ones. Given this diversity, the results need to be standardized for ease of understanding.

Some Sample Company Examples

To assist in following the implications of what can be a challenging set of analyses, the profit results of three different firms will be presented at various points throughout the report. Those three firms are (1) a low-margin, low-expense, high-asset utilization firm, (2) a mid-range margin, expense and asset utilization firm and (3) a high-margin, high-expense, low-asset utilization firm. Despite their important operating differences, all three firms start with an ROA of around 8.0%.

The 8.0% ROA was not chosen randomly. This represents the typical performance of distribution companies reporting results to the Profit Planning Group through its benchmarking programs. In point of fact, a 7.0% to 8.0% ROA has been the longer-term norm in distribution for many years.[3]

Their relative profit positions are shown in **Exhibit 1**. It should be noted that all three firms have been assigned a sales volume of $10.0 million as a starting point. This is done to ease the analytical process. In point of fact, firms with such diverse operating models would have very different sales levels. Assigning them the same sales volume simplifies the analysis. In no way does it change the conclusions that can be drawn.

Many readers will argue that $10.0 million is a small number in today's distribution marketplace. It was chosen so that the impact of making changes in the CPVs

---

3   The first documentation of the long-term consistency in ROA can be found in Albert D. Bates, *Profit Myths in Wholesale Distribution*, NAW Institute for Distribution Excellence, 2007.

Exhibit 1
The Financial Structure of a Sample Firm
in Three Different Industries

	Low Gross Margin and Expenses	Medium Gross Margin and Expenses	High Gross Margin and Expenses
Income Statement ($)			
Net Sales	$10,000,000	$10,000,000	$10,000,000
Cost of Goods Sold	9,000,000	8,000,000	7,000,000
Gross Margin	10% 1,000,000	20% 2,000,000	30% 3,000,000
Expenses			
Payroll and Fringe Benefits	575,000	1,100,000	1,750,000
All Other Expenses	325,000	650,000	900,000
Total Expenses	9% 900,000	1,750,000	2,650,000
Profit Before Taxes	$100,000	$250,000	$350,000
Income Statement (%)			
Net Sales	100.0	100.0	100.0
Cost of Goods Sold	90.0	80.0	70.0
Gross Margin	10.0	20.0	30.0
Expenses			
Payroll and Fringe Benefits	5.8 %	11.0	17.5
All Other Expenses	3.3	6.5	9.0
Total Expenses	9.0 %	17.5	26.5
Profit Before Taxes	1.0	2.5	3.5
Asset Investment			
Accounts Receivable	$400,000	$825,000	$1,350,000
Inventory	450,000	2,000,000	2,350,000
All Other Asssets	400,000	300,000	675,000
Total Assets	$1,250,000	$3,125,000	$4,375,000
Asset Utilization Ratios			
Inventory Turnover (times)	20.0	4.0	3.0
Days Sales Outstanding (days)	14.6	30.1	49.3
Return on Assets	8.0%	8.0%	8.0%

= PBT ÷ total assets

could be identified easily. All of the concepts presented here work for larger firms in the same exact way as demonstrated in the text.

Not only do firms in different lines of trade have different sales, margin and expenses; they also have different rates of ROA. For illustrative purposes, though, an 8.0% ROA is a very legitimate starting point as most—but certainly not all—distribution industries are relatively close to this 8.0% ROA level.

One final point should be noted regarding Exhibit 1. In every line of trade expenses are heavily weighted towards payroll and fringe benefits. Typically somewhere around two-thirds of all expenses are comprised of payroll, payroll taxes, insurance and retirement benefits. Distribution is a service-heavy business. Since services are provided by people, it is also a payroll-heavy business. This reality will be important in the analysis of expenses.

Structure of the Report

The report is organized into sections which parallel the CPVs.

- **Sales**—An analysis of the impact of both sales size (relative to the firm's peers in its line of trade) and the relative level of sales growth.
- **Gross Margin and Expenses**—An examination of the two key operating metrics in distribution.
- **Investment**—A review of both inventory turnover and DSO as determinants of profitability.
- **The Profit Sweet Spot**—A discussion of how the CPVs might be combined to produce dramatically higher levels of profitability.
- **Implications for Action**—Guidelines on how to follow through on the conclusions of the report.

By design this report is concerned much more with what to do than how to do it. That is, it will suggest how changing the CPVs causes either PBT or ROA to increase or decrease. However, it can make only limited suggestions as to how the improvements in the CPVs might be generated.

Even with that caveat, knowing what actions improve profitability for a large group of distributors is invaluable. It should provide a starting point for enhancing results in every firm.

■ Section Two:
Sales as a CPV

As every manager knows, a reasonable level of sales volume is required for success. However, there is uncertainty as to exactly how much sales volume is required for that success. Despite the lack of precise measurements, there is universal agreement that sales is a critical CPV. In point of fact, sales really constitutes two distinct CPVs. The first is the magnitude of the sales, the second is the rate of sales growth.

Sales volume and sales growth share one common attribute that is important in the analysis. Namely, they incorporate the largest variations in results of all of the CPVs. In the overall sample, specifically, sales volume ranges from just above $1.0 million to over $5.0 billion. Any generalizations regarding sales volume must be able to represent a wide swath of firms.

There is a similar, but narrower, degree of variation with regard to sales growth. On the low end sales growth cannot fall below -100.0%, while the upper end again has no realistic limit. In the overall sample the range observed was from -25.0% to +100.0%.

How Sales Impacts Profitability

The potential positive relationship between dollar sales volume and profitability comes from two factors. First, larger firms can buy more advantageously, which should have a positive impact on gross margin. Second, economies of scale should push operating expense percentages down.

These clear advantages are frequently offset by mirror-image disadvantages. Larger firms are often price aggressive in order to ensure that they really do remain larger than typical. On the expense side, economies of scale sometimes morph into diseconomies of bureaucracy as the firm reaches a very large size.

Sales growth has a somewhat similar yin and yang nature. Fast growing firms can increase their sales against the underlying growth rate in expenses which is usually tied to the parallel rate of inflation. Offsetting this, high levels of growth tend to push the firm beyond its financial and operating capacity and profits suffer.

The net result is that both sales volume and sales growth need to be analyzed as potential double-edge swords. High levels of sales or sales growth may be either positive or negative.

The Impact of Sales Size

Dollar sales volume is unique among the CPVs in that it is very difficult for a firm to change its relative position quickly. A $5.0 million sales firm, as an illustration, can't simply decide to become a $5.0 billion one next year. Firms can experience sales increases or decreases each year, of course. However, a very small firm this year is likely to still be a very small one next year even if it grows rapidly during the interim. Similarly, a very large firm is likely to remain a very large one.

The inability to change *relative* sales quickly colors the results. Any impact of sales volume on profit must reflect existing operating realities more than immediate opportunities for action. That is, if small firms are disadvantaged in terms of producing high levels of profit, it is something small firms must live with and work around. Even with this caveat, it is valuable to know where those operating realities lie.

In analyzing the impact of dollar sales volume, two different analytical approaches, or tests, will be employed. These same tests will be used in subsequent sections for gross margin, expenses and investment factors. This necessitates some additional discussion of methodology here.

High/Low Test—The first, and more simplistic, test is to determine if sales volume makes any difference at the most aggregate level. The question here is simply do larger firms generate better profits than smaller ones? The question is addressed by comparing the half of the firms that are larger than their peers in their line of trade with the half that are smaller.

Even though this is a simple test, it produces an important finding. Larger firms really are more profitable than smaller ones (measured against peers in the same line of trade, not against the overall sample). Larger firms have an ROA that is 15.9% higher than the industry norm, while smaller firms have an ROA that is 23.9% lower. It is a large difference. The economies of scale more than offset the diseconomies of bureaucracy.

It should be recalled that all three of the sample firms developed in Section One have a base ROA of 8.0%. This reflects the median profit performance of distribution firms in the benchmarking studies used as the basis for this analysis. The results suggest the top half of the firms in terms of sales size operate on an ROA of 9.3% (8.0% x 1.159) simply because they are larger. The firms in the bottom half have an ROA of 6.1% (8.0% x [1 - .239]). It must once again be emphasized that large means compared to other firms in a specific line of trade.

The relative impact of sales on PBT is almost exactly the same as the impact on ROA. Specifically, small firms have a PBT that is 23.3% below their industry medians, while large firms have a PBT that is 17.4% higher. The ROA and PBT impacts were very similar in character.

This is not an inconsequential finding. The underlying implication is that sales size impacts gross margin and expenses, but does not appear to have an influence on asset utilization. If size did have an asset impact (probably via more effective control of inventory and accounts receivable) then the ROA impact would be larger than the PBT impact. Sales volume has a profit influence but not an investment influence.

All three of the sample firms from Section One have the same ROA, but they have differing PBT numbers because of their differing margin and expense structures. The impact of sales volume on PBT reflects those differences:

Sales Size Category	PBT (%)		
	Low Margin/ Low Expenses	Mid-Range Margin/Expenses	High Margin/ High Expenses
Sample Firms	1.0	2.5	3.5
Small Size	0.8	1.9	2.7
Large Size	1.2	2.9	4.1

Continuous Improvement Test—The second test is to break the firms into the quintiles discussed earlier. The issue under investigation here is whether size appears to have a consistent impact on profitability. Specifically, does every quintile have a higher ROA or PBT than the previous one? Each quintile will contain good and bad performers, of course. However, the real question is does continuous improvement with regard to sales size result in continuous improvement with regard to profitability?

Before examining the results, a reminder regarding the composition of those quintiles is necessary. By definition, each group contains 20.0% of the sample or about 177 firms. The quintiles for Sales Size are as follows (with all comparisons relative to the results for the firm's specific line of trade):

- **Very Small**—More than 60.0% smaller.
- **Small**—Between 20.0% and 60.0% smaller.
- **Mid-Range**—Between 20.0% smaller and 25.0% larger.
- **Large**—Between 25.0% and 120.0% larger.
- **Very Large**—More than 120.0% larger.

This means that in an industry where the typical firm generates $10.0 million in sales volume, the Very Small category includes all of the firms with sales of $4.0 million or less. The Very Large group includes firms with sales of at least $22.0 million. As noted several times, the diversity of sales results, even in a single line of trade, is substantial.

Exhibit 2 is the first of a series of graphs that reflects the impact of the CPVs on both PBT and ROA. As can be seen, there is a pronounced difference in profitability due to sales size, with profit increasing consistently as relative sales volume rises.

The lone exception is at the small end of the sales range. It appears that the profit challenge is not just in being in the first quintile comprised of the smallest firms. Instead, it is associated with being in either the first or second quintile. Being very small doesn't make the profit challenge any less severe than simply being small. All of the smaller firms face the same profit hurdles.

It is also worth noting that all of the small firms are not doomed to produce low profits. Some small firms can, and do, produce strong profits. It is just that statistically the odds are stacked against them.

The implications of Exhibit 2 in terms of ROA and PBT can be calculated easily for the illustrative firms. The word illustrative should always be top of mind—there is no absolute relationship as every firm is unique. The results indicate how sales size tends to impact profit.

The ROA results are straightforward. Each of the three sample firms is set at an 8.0% ROA to reflect the overall profit performance in distribution. From that baseline ROA is impacted by sales size in the following manner:

Sales Size Category	ROA (%)
Sample Firms	8.0
Very Small	5.7
Small	5.4
Mid-Range	8.6
Large	9.1
Very Large	9.9

As noted previously, the PBT numbers are very different for the three sample firms reflecting the different gross margin and expense structures of their lines of trade. Consequently, three sets of parallel results are produced for PBT:

Sales Size Category	PBT (%)		
	Low Margin/ Low Expenses	Mid-Range Margin/Expenses	High Margin/ High Expenses
Sample Firms	1.0	2.5	3.5
Very Small	0.7	1.8	2.5
Small	0.7	1.7	2.4
Mid-Range	1.1	2.6	3.7
Large	1.1	2.8	4.0
Very Large	1.3	3.3	4.6

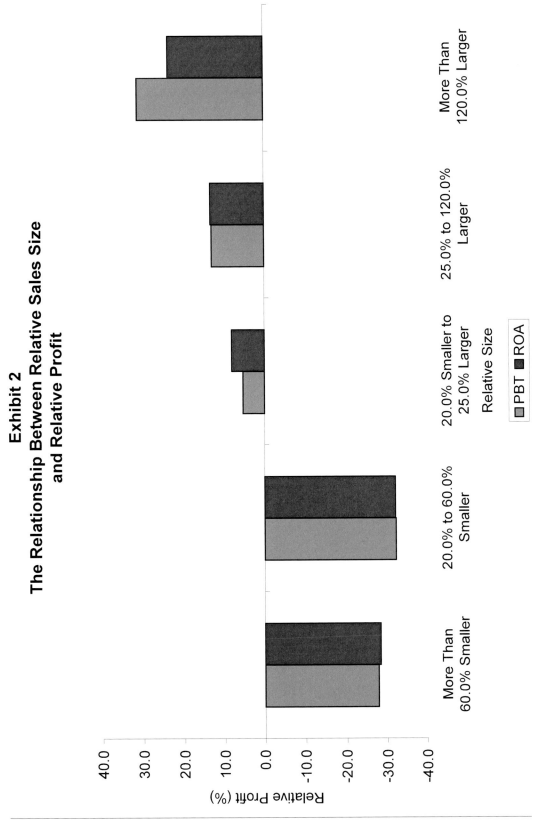

Exhibit 2
The Relationship Between Relative Sales Size
and Relative Profit

The global implication for smaller firms is that there may be no real advantage in trying to become incrementally larger. However, if a small firm could get relatively close to the typical firm (say $8.0 million in sales if $10.0 million is typical), then it would begin to have the resources to increase its odds of generating higher profit.

The overall implication for larger firms is that the economies of scale appear to outweigh the diseconomies. Moving to a large volume category over time should provide a profitability benefit.

The quintiles in Exhibit 2 leave one important question unanswered. That question revolves around the fact that the mid-range quintile includes firms that are both somewhat smaller and somewhat larger than the industry norm.

The obvious question is whether the slightly smaller firms have profit results that are appreciably different than firms that are slightly larger. The answer is a definitive no. The two subsets of close-to-typical firms (slightly smaller/slightly larger) are very similar in terms of profitability, considering both PBT and ROA.

The implications of the two tests, taken in conjunction, are extremely important. Larger firms have an important advantage over smaller ones in terms of generating profit. The challenge associated with being small is universal for both the first and second quintile. However, the advantage of being larger is only pronounced when firms move into the fifth quintile in their industry.

It is worth reiterating, though, that large sales size is no absolute guarantee of success. Large firms can produce a miniscule profit and small firms can produce a huge profit. Large firms simply have an advantage in the quest.

The Impact of Sales Growth

Sales growth rates vary significantly between different firms, although not nearly as much as absolute sales dollars. As was mentioned earlier, the range (excluding a few outliers) is -25.0% to +100.0%. Overall, the growth rate for firms in the report is right at 7.0%, including inflation. This reflects the performance of a mature sector of the economy. The 7.0% overall growth rate will be used in subsequent calculations to put the underlying actual growth rates into context.

Unlike relative sales size, relative sales growth is a somewhat-controllable CPV. If rapid sales growth has a positive impact, then moving from 5.0% growth to 10.0% growth would be desirable, regardless of the absolute level of sales. The two tests suggest there are some outstanding opportunities associated with sales growth.

High/Low Test—Once again using the more simplistic of the tests, faster-growing firms are more profitable than slower-growing ones (growth being measured against peers in the same line of trade). Faster-growing firms have an ROA that is 23.6% higher than the industry norm, while slower-growing ones have an ROA that is 18.5% lower.

As a reminder, all three of the sample firms shown in Section One have an ROA of 8.0%. The results mean that the top half of the firms in terms of sales growth operate on an ROA of 9.9% due to their superior sales growth. The firms in the bottom half have an ROA of only 6.5%.

The structure of the results is similar to that for sales volume. Just as larger is more profitable with regard to sales size, faster is more profitable with regard to sales growth. However, the profit penalty from slower growth is less than the penalty for low sales volume while the profit bonus from rapid growth is significantly greater than the bonus for having a larger sales volume. Stated in more direct terms, slow growth hurts a little; rapid growth helps a lot.

The relative impact of sales growth on PBT tracks very closely to the impact on ROA. As with sales volume, the profit impact of sales growth is concentrated on factors that influence the bottom line rather than factors that influence investment. As before, it is possible to demonstrate the impact on PBT for the three sample firms. The impact of sales growth on PBT for the three firms is as follows:

Sales Growth Category	PBT (%)		
	Low Margin/ Low Expenses	Mid-Range Margin/Expenses	High Margin/ High Expenses
Sample Firms	1.0	2.5	3.5
Slow Growth	0.8	2.1	3.0
Fast Growth	1.2	3.0	4.2

Continuous Improvement Test—No company's sales growth can fall below -100.0% except for one year. In the sample almost no firms fell below -25.0%. There is no upper limit to sales growth, but only a few companies in the sample grew faster than 100.0%.

Consequently, the Sales Growth quintiles are as follows:
- **Very Slow**—More than 120.0% slower.
- **Slow**—Between 40.0% and 120.0% slower.
- **Mid-Range**—Between 40.0% slower and 40.0% faster.
- **Fast**—Between 40.0% and 150.0% faster.
- **Very Fast**—More than 150.0% faster.

At first blush these differences in growth rates appear huge with a range of -120.0% to +150.0%. In fact, the differences are relatively small in the third quintile, and large only at the extremes. Understanding the magnitude of the relative growth rates is made easier by looking at the implications for actual growth.

The third group, with a ± 40.0% relative growth rate, has an actual sales growth rate between 4.2% (7.0% x .6) and 9.8% (7.0% x 1.4). Clearly, this is a measurable difference from the overall rate of 7.0%. However, it is nothing compared to the first and fifth quintiles.

A 150.0% delta in growth for the fastest growing group translates to a sales growth rate of 17.5%. At the other extreme a relative growth rate of -120.0% means that sales *declined* by 1.4%. This means a $10.0 million firm in the previous year would have increased its sales base to $11.75 million in the fastest-growing group. Conversely sales would have declined to $9.86 million in the slowest-growing quintile.

Exhibit 3 reflects the large differences in profitability associated with sales growth. Profitability—as measured by either ROA or PBT—increases at every step from slower growth to faster growth. In all cases the penalty or reward associated with sales growth is larger for PBT than it is for ROA. This tends to suggest that additional asset investments precede the increase in sales.

The implications of Exhibit 3 in terms of ROA and PBT are crucial given that sales growth is not a structural factor, but a controllable CPV. The ROA difference between the slowest-growing and fastest-growing quintiles is nearly double.

Sales Growth Category	ROA (%)
Sample Firms	8.0
Very Slow	5.5
Slow	7.2
Mid-Range	8.0
Fast	9.4
Very Fast	10.8

Once again, the PBT numbers are very different for the three illustrative firms reflecting the gross margin and expense structure of their lines of trade. Consequently, three sets of parallel results are produced for PBT.

Sales Growth Category	PBT (%)		
	Low Margin/ Low Expenses	Mid-Range Margin/Expenses	High Margin/ High Expenses
Sample Firms	1.0	2.5	3.5
Very Slow	0.7	1.7	2.3
Slow	0.9	2.2	3.1
Mid-Range	1.1	2.6	3.7
Fast	1.2	2.9	4.1
Very Fast	1.4	3.4	4.8

The quintiles, as in the past, leave one question unanswered. Do the firms that grow slightly faster than the industry norm do better than the ones that grow slightly slower? The third, or middle, quintile includes firms growing 40.0% slower than the typical firm to ones growing 40.0% faster. Does being on the positive side of the mid-range group make a difference versus being on the negative side?

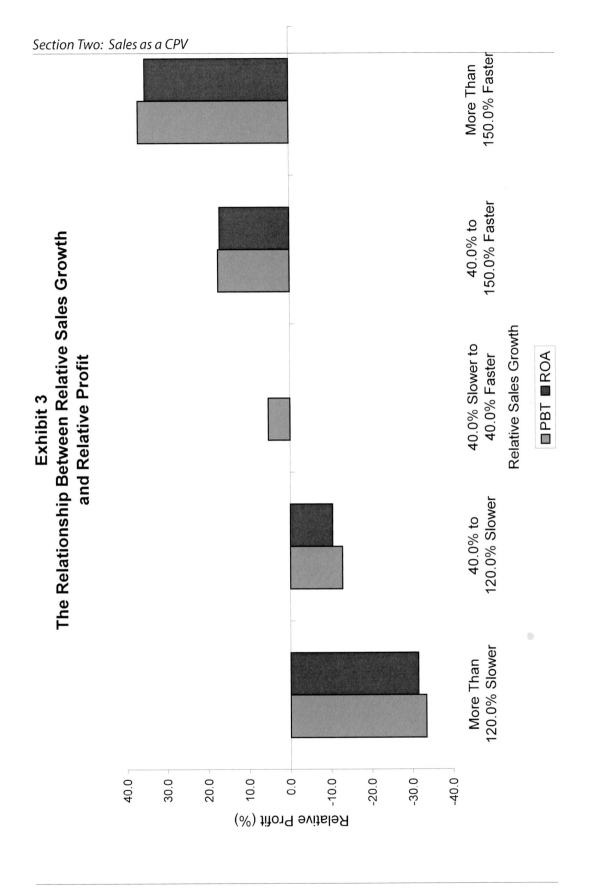

Exhibit 3
The Relationship Between Relative Sales Growth
and Relative Profit

The answer is yes, to a degree. The difference between slightly slow and slightly fast is worth about 1.0 percentage point in terms of ROA. It is measurable, but pales in comparison to moving to the next quintile on sales growth.

As was the case with sales volume, sales growth is not an absolute guarantee of success. Very rapid sales growth provides a profitability advantage while very slow sales growth tends to retard profitability. Profits for firms that are relatively close to the industry sales growth rate are impacted only marginally.

While rapid growth provides an important advantage in the quest for strong profit levels, growth alone is not enough. Slow-growth firms have the potential to overcome the growth disadvantage with rigorous dedication to the other CPVs. Fast-growth firms can squander the growth advantage.

Conclusions Regarding Sales

Both the level of sales and the sales growth rate have strong relationships to profitability, as measured in terms of either PBT or ROA. However, the two sales factors impact profit results in somewhat different ways.

Sales size is a particular problem for smaller firms. The bottom 40.0% of the firms (the first two quintiles) experience very low levels of profit performance. However, the inherent inability to quickly and easily change the firm's size diminishes the power of sales volume as a tool in improving results for smaller firms in the short run.

Among firms in the mid-to-upper ranges of sales size, the relationship between sales and profitability is direct and strong. Even here there is something of a "nothing much can be done about it" perspective. Firms could certainly engage in merger and acquisition activity to gain additional scale. However, the lack of an absolute correlation between sales size and profitability could well diminish enthusiasm for such actions.

Sales growth has a much stronger and much more direct relationship to profitability. Given that sales growth is a CPV than can be impacted through management actions, it should probably prove to be the primary sales focus for most management teams.

In financial and marketing planning, firms should probably think in terms of setting a specific sales growth goal. Even so, sales growth provides no guarantee of success.

■ Section Three:
Gross Margin and Operating Expenses as CPVs

With both sales volume and sales growth there are extremely large variations in performance. Sales volume ranges from $1.0 million to $5.0 billion and sales growth ranges from -25.0% to +100.0%.

In very sharp contrast the variations in the gross margin percentage (again relative to the industry norm) and the operating expense percentage are modest. This means that any potential impact these factors have on profit will be noticeable even if the margin and expenses differences are small.

In reviewing the potential impact of margin and expenses, one other important factor emerges. Across different lines of trade, gross margin and operating expenses tend to move in direct relationship to each other. Low gross margin industries are also low operating expense industries.

This clearly defined congruence between gross margin and operating expense percentages across different lines of trade generally holds within lines of trade as well. Firms with a high gross margin percentage almost inevitably have a high operating expense percentage.

One explanation for this is that firms with high gross margin percentages provide a lot of services in support of that gross margin and thus have higher operating expenses. The opposite perspective is that firms with high expenses by necessity must generate higher gross margin percentages. In either case, the two variables are strongly linked.

As a result of the linkage there is a tendency to think of gross margin and operating expense percentages as being simply two parts of the same profit driver. That perspective does not hold true when the empirical evidence is reviewed. The real key to success is the ability to modify the linkage. That is, success comes from a high gross margin percentage and only a *somewhat* higher operating expense percentage or a low operating expense percentage and a *somewhat* lower gross margin percentage.

Gross Margin and Operating Expenses Correlation

Statistically, about 85.0% of the variation in operating expense percentages can be explained by variations in the gross margin percentage. Stated in the opposite manner, about 85.0% of the difference in gross margin percentages can be explained by differences in operating expense percentages.

To get technical momentarily, the regression coefficient relating gross margin and operating expenses is .8525 (see the Appendix for more detail). The two factors definitely track together. Even with 85.0% of the variation accounted for, that still leaves 15.0% unexplained. It is this difference that separates typical firms from the top or bottom ones.

As noted above some firms can modify the linkage between gross margin and operating expenses. Some are able to increase their gross margin percentage a lot while their operating expense percentage goes up only a little. Other firms have a slightly lower gross margin percentage with a lower operating expense percentage.

Of greater consequence, a few firms within an individual industry actually are able to break the linkage entirely. They are able to combine a high gross margin percentage (relative to the industry norm) with a low operating expense percentage. They are, by definition, the highest of the high-profit firms. At the other extreme, some firms combine a low margin percentage with a high expense percentage to produce inordinately low profit.

It is this variation between the two factors that should interest management. Consequently, gross margin and operating expenses will be viewed as separate entities in this section. They are separate CPVs.

The Impact of Gross Margin

The same two tests that were applied to sales volume and sales growth will also be applied to the gross margin percentage here and to the operating expense percentage later in Section Three. As a reminder, those two tests are (1) a simple test of high versus low margin and expenses and (2) an evaluation of the quintiles.

High/Low Test—The results of the first test indicate that high-gross margin firms are more profitable than low-gross margin ones (gross margin as measured against peers in the same line of trade, not against the overall sample). The impact is less pronounced than for either sales size or sales growth. The firms with a high gross margin percentage have an ROA that is 11.2% higher than the industry norm. The firms with a low gross margin percentage have an ROA that is 10.3% lower.

It should be remembered that all three of the sample firms developed in Section One have an ROA of 8.0%. This means that the top half of the firms in terms of gross margin produce an ROA of 9.0% (8.0% x 1.112). This is generated on the same level of sales, but combined with a higher margin. The firms in the bottom half have an ROA of 7.1% (8.0% x [1 - .103]).

The relative impact of gross margin on PBT is almost exactly the same as the impact on ROA. The impact on PBT for the three illustrative firms is as follows:

Gross Margin Category	PBT (%)		
	Low Margin/ Low Expenses	Mid-Range Margin/Expenses	High Margin/ High Expenses
Sample Firms	1.0	2.5	3.5
Low Margin	0.9	2.3	3.2
High Margin	1.2	3.0	4.1

Continuous Improvement Test—When the high/low analysis is supplanted by the quintile analysis, the results highlight a relationship between gross margin and improved profitability that is fairly consistent. However, the penalty for having a low gross margin percentage is structurally different from the reward for having a high one.

The Gross Margin quintiles used for the analysis (with all figures versus industry peers) are:

- **Very Low**—More than 12.5% lower.
- **Low**—Between 3.0% and 12.5% lower.
- **Mid-Range**—Between 3.0% lower and 3.5% higher.
- **High**—Between 3.5% and 15.0% higher.
- **Very High**—More than 15.0% higher.

The quintiles regarding gross margin percentage have to be interpreted on an industry-by-industry basis. The three sample companies established in Section One greatly facilitate that process.

For the low-gross margin firm (10.0% GM) the first quintile (the lowest) has a gross margin below 8.8% (10.0% x [1 - .125]). The fifth quintile has a gross margin of at least 11.5% (10.0% x 1.15). This margin difference exists even though the high-quintile and low-quintile firms operate in the same line of trade.

For the mid-range line of trade (20.0% GM) the gross margin levels for the upper and lower quintiles are 17.5% and 23.0%. Finally for the high-margin industry (30.0% GM) the figures are 26.3% and 34.5% respectively.

Exhibit 4 visualizes the relationship between gross margin and both PBT and ROA. The relationship is reasonably direct. The real exceptions, as suggested earlier, are at the high and low ends of the spectrum.

At the low end, the first and second quintiles suffer to about the same degree with regard to both ROA and PBT. Firms with a very low gross margin don't perform any worse than those with simply a low gross margin. However, both groups do perform demonstrably worse than any other quintile.

For the fifth quintile, PBT literally explodes, but ROA actually declines compared to the previous quintile. This may well indicate that exceptionally high levels of gross margin can only be reached through a significant investment in inventory. This could come through purchasing larger quantities in normal operations or through extensive advance buying when such opportunities arise.

The implication for low-gross margin firms is that the direct correlation noted earlier between gross margin and expenses absolutely must be broken. Lower-margin firms must be even more expense-control aggressive than they are at present or they must move to a higher-margin position.

For high-margin firms the implication appears to be one of investment control. The increase in margin must be achieved without the significant investment commitments that are required to reach the higher level.

The ROA calculation is straightforward as the three sample firms have all been set at an 8.0% ROA. As a reminder, the 8.0% figure represents the overall profit performance in distribution.

Gross Margin Category	ROA (%)
Sample Firms	8.0
Very Low	6.9
Low	6.5
Mid-Range	9.1
High	8.8
Very High	8.2

Once again the PBT numbers are very different for the three illustrative firms reflecting the gross margin and expense structure of their lines of trade. Consequently, three sets of parallel results are produced for PBT.

Gross Margin Category	PBT (%)		
	Low Margin/ Low Expenses	Mid-Range Margin/Expenses	High Margin/ High Expenses
Sample Firms	1.0	2.5	3.5
Very Low	0.9	2.2	3.1
Low	0.8	2.1	3.0
Mid-Range	1.1	2.8	3.9
High	1.1	2.8	3.9
Very High	1.2	3.1	4.4

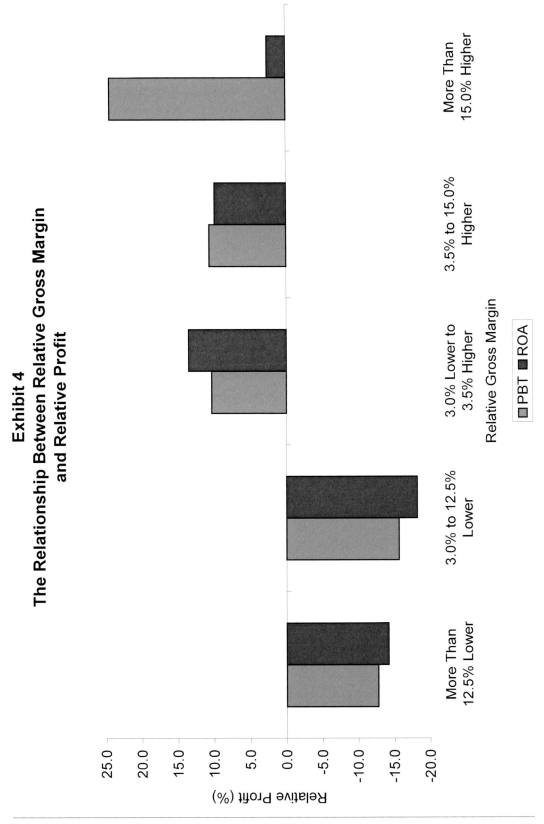

Exhibit 4
The Relationship Between Relative Gross Margin and Relative Profit

The quintiles in Exhibit 4 leave the same unanswered question as in the previous section. The mid-range quintile includes firms that are both slightly below and slightly above the gross margin norm for their line of trade. Is there a difference between "just above" and "just below" the typical gross margin percentage?

The answer is decidedly yes. Thinking back to sales volume and sales growth for a moment, the only requirement was to be close to typical. There was no advantage from being either slightly above or below the typical number.

However, for gross margin, being just below typical or just above typical creates two very different profit positions. Firms slightly below the industry norm for gross margin have a PBT that is about 4.0% lower than the typical firm. Firms with a slightly higher than typical gross margin enjoy a PBT that is more than 20.0% higher than the typical firm. The ROA results are almost identical, with low-gross margin firms 4.8% below the industry norm and high-gross margin ones 23.6% above the norm.

All of this supports the conclusion that gross margin must be managed as an independent profit variable. This is true even though gross margin and operating expenses are highly correlated. Higher is decidedly better than lower. Even slightly higher is significantly better.

The Impact of Operating Expenses

Expense control is almost every manager's least favorite topic. Cutting expenses implies going backwards while increasing sales is moving forward. Expense control is almost admitting defeat in the competitive arena.

Despite its lack of popularity, operating expenses represent a highly-controllable CPV. Controlling expenses is also the one CPV action that can be taken irrespective of either suppliers or customers. To increase sales, customers have to buy more. To increase gross margin suppliers have to lower their prices or customers have to pay more, or both. In contrast, expense control can be a unilateral action.

The two tests also suggest that expense control is the *single most important driver of profitability*. That statement should help offset the lack of popularity of expense control. Minimizing expense control is a losing proposition.

High/Low Test—Expense control produces the largest and most direct impact on both PBT and ROA of any of the CPVs. The half of the firms with a lower operating expense percentage (measured against peers in the same line of trade) enjoy a 30.0% increase in both ratios. Firms with higher operating expenses have an almost exactly opposite 30.0% decline in both profitability ratios. No other CPV comes close to producing this result.

Using the baseline 8.0% ROA ratio for all of distribution, the result is pronounced. The top half with lower operating expenses produces an ROA of 10.4% simply due to expense control. Meanwhile, the bottom half operates on an ROA of only 5.6%.

There is close to a doubling of ROA in moving from a high-expense structure to a low-expense one.

The relative impact of expense control on PBT tracks almost identically with the impact on ROA. The specific impact on PBT for the three sample firms is as follows:

Operating Expense Category	PBT (%)		
	Low Margin/ Low Expenses	Mid-Range Margin/Expenses	High Margin/ High Expenses
Sample Firms	1.0	2.5	3.5
High Expenses	0.7	1.7	2.4
Low Expenses	1.3	3.3	4.6

Continuous Improvement Test—The expense curve skews very slightly towards higher expense ratios. No company's operating expense percentage can be more than 100.0% below its peers. There is no upper limit on how high operating expense percentages can be versus the industry norm. As a practical matter, though, ±20.0% represents a huge variation in the operating expense ratio.

Given this narrow range, the Operating Expense Percentage quintiles are as follows:

- **Very High**—More than 20.0% higher.
- **High**—Between 5.0% and 20.0% higher.
- **Mid-Range**—Between 5.0% higher and 5.0% lower.
- **Low**—Between 5.0% and 17.5% lower.
- **Very Low**—More than 17.5% lower.

The range of operating expense variations is very close to the range on the gross margin percentage. This is because, as mentioned at the start of this section, operating expenses and gross margin are highly correlated.

Despite that correlation, **Exhibit 5** is very different than any graph seen before. The relationship is startlingly direct. Moving towards the right, every quintile does better with regard to profit than the preceding quintile.

The impact is also exceptionally pronounced. Low-expense firms don't just do better, they do a lot better. The scale of the graph ranges from 60.0% lower profit to 80.0% higher profit, the widest spread associated with any graph in the study. This is the only CPV for which every quintile performs better than the previous one and the differences are dramatic.

As with gross margin, the operating expense percentage quintiles have to be interpreted on an industry-by-industry basis. The three sample companies established in Section One greatly facilitate that process.

For the low margin/low expense firm (9.0% operating expense percentage) the highest quintile indicates an operating expense percentage in excess of 10.8%

(9.0% x 1.2). The lowest-expense quintile has an operating expense percentage of less than 7.4% or better. Once again differences exist even though the high and low-quintile firms operate in the same line of trade.

For the mid-range sample firm (17.5% operating expense percentage) the expense percentages for the first and fifth quintiles are 21.0% and 14.4% respectively. Finally for the high margin/high expense firm (26.5% operating expense percentage) the figures are 31.8% and 21.9%.

The massive differences in the expense structure do not fall directly to the bottom line, of course. As noted twice before, firms with low operating expense percentages also tend to have a low gross margin which eats into the advantage. High expense firms get some relief through higher gross margins.

Having said that, Exhibit 5 outlines very directly that expense control drives both ROA and PBT at a very rapid rate. The implications of Exhibit 5 are crucial given that expenses represent a highly-controllable CPV. In addition, the ROA difference between the worst and best expense quintiles is nearly 3.5 times.

Operating Expense Category	ROA (%)
Sample Firms	8.0
Very High	3.7
High	6.5
Mid-Range	8.9
Low	10.3
Very Low	12.9

Once again, the PBT numbers are very different for the three illustrative firms reflecting alternative gross margin and expense structures. Consequently, three sets of parallel results are produced for PBT.

Operating Expense Category	PBT (%)		
	Low Margin/ Low Expenses	Mid-Range Margin/Expenses	High Margin/ High Expenses
Sample Firms	1.0	2.5	3.5
Very High	0.5	1.2	1.7
High	0.8	1.9	2.7
Mid-Range	1.0	2.4	3.4
Low	1.3	3.4	4.7
Very Low	1.5	3.8	5.3

Finally, there remains the issue of whether the third quintile should be considered as two distinct groups. Specifically, do profit results differ for firms with slightly lower operating expenses versus those with slightly higher?

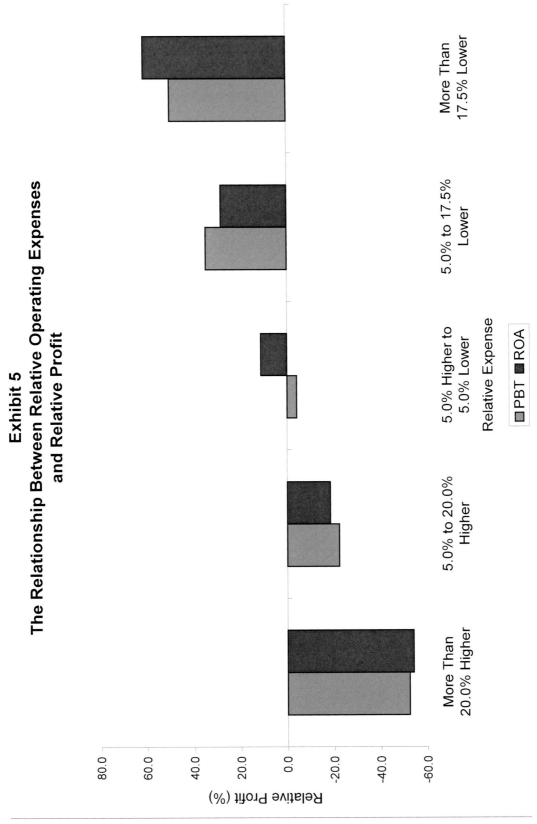

Exhibit 5
The Relationship Between Relative Operating Expenses and Relative Profit

The answer is a definite no. Firms within 5.0% of industry-norm expense levels have virtually identical profit results. This is true for both ROA and PBT.

The Payroll Component of Operating Expenses

As was stated in Section One of this report, payroll (including all fringe benefits) is by far the single largest operating expense for virtually every distribution firm. In every line of trade in this sample, payroll accounts for somewhere between 60.0% and 70.0% of total operating expenses. As a practical matter it is impossible to control operating expenses without controlling payroll.

The impact of payroll can be understood very quickly by reviewing **Exhibit 6** which presents the quintile analysis for payroll and profitability. The exhibit is an almost exact duplicate of Exhibit 5 which looked at total operating expenses and profitability.

The only major difference between Exhibits 5 and 6 is the scale. For total expenses in Exhibit 5 the scale for profit variations is -60.0% to +80.0%. In Exhibit 6 the scale is a less dramatic -40.0% to +60.0%. As noted, payroll is somewhere between 60.0% and 70.0% of total operating expenses in every line of trade in the research project. As a result, payroll accounts for about the same percent of the overall impact of operating expenses on profit.

Conclusions Regarding
Gross Margin and Operating Expenses

Both the gross margin percentage and the operating expense percentage have a strong relationship to profitability, whether measured in terms of PBT or ROA. However, the two factors impact profit results in very different ways.

Gross margin has a direct relationship to profit. However, the penalty for having a low gross margin appears to be greater than the reward for having a high one. The margin-to-profit relationship becomes strained when examining ROA for the very high-gross margin firms.

Expenses, in very sharp contrast, appear to impact both PBT and ROA directly in all cases under almost any set of circumstances that can be imagined. It is the most direct driver of profitability among all of the CPVs.

Because of the importance of payroll in the overall mix of operating expenses it also has a very strong relationship to both ROA and PBT. No expense-control effort is going to succeed without considering payroll.

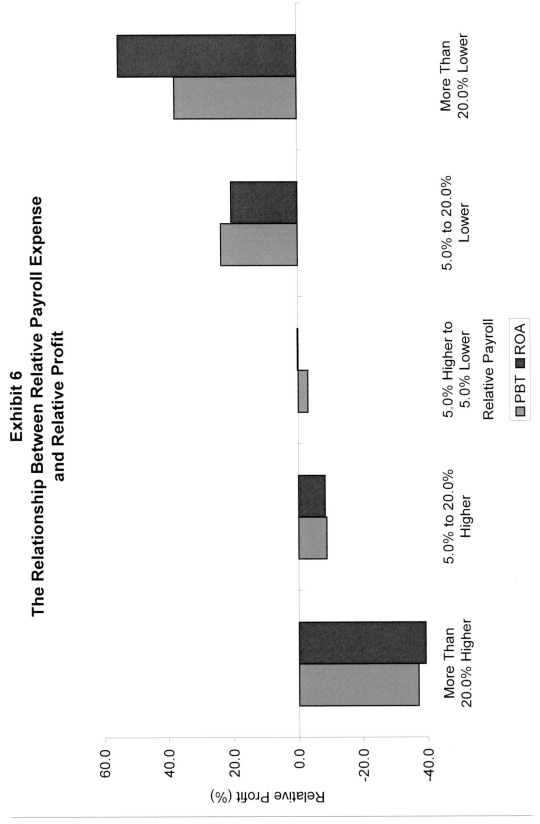

Exhibit 6
The Relationship Between Relative Payroll Expense and Relative Profit

■ Section Four:
Accounts Receivable and Inventory as CPVs

One of the financial realities throughout distribution is that the typical firm does not have a lot of cash. Instead, distributors have a lot of accounts receivable and inventory. The profit that is generated each year tends to be reinvested back into additional accounts receivable and additional inventory. This probably has been true for as long as there have been distributors.

During the last dozen years or so this scenario of lots of accounts receivable and inventory but not much cash has become more acute. The severe economic downturn of 2002 (caused by the events of 2001) made the lack of cash a much more pressing concern. The brutally severe recession of 2009 aggravated the problem even further.

It is not an overstatement to say that distributors have made a collective commitment to never run out of cash again. That commitment translates operationally into a desire to lower inventory (therefore increasing inventory turnover) and lower accounts receivable (reducing the days sales outstanding—the DSO). The reduction in these two asset categories serves to increase cash balances and provides a cushion against future sales challenges.

The rush to increase the inventory turnover and lower the DSO has exposed the fact that both accounts receivable and inventory are very much double-edged swords. With lowered inventory levels the likelihood of a reduced service level becomes acute.

Similarly, reducing lines of credit to customers also has the potential to impact sales in a negative way, although not to the same extent as reducing inventory. Since sales growth was identified as an important CPV in Section Two, the logic of lowering investment can be called into question if it causes sales to suffer.

This section will look specifically at the issue of whether inventory turnover and the DSO have a so-called "Goldilocks" level of investment. That means trying to find a point at which there is enough investment to generate adequate sales without tying up excessive amounts of capital.

Limited Intra-Industry Variation

Like the other CPVs, there is a wide range of variability across different lines of trade with regard to the key investment categories. Inventory turnover levels range from 3.0 times in some industries to over 20.0 times in others. Similarly, the DSO can be as low as 15.0 days and as high as 60.0 days. These inter-industry variations reflect both historical and structural differences between industries.

Once the analysis narrows to a single line of trade, though, the variations tend to diminish very rapidly. For both the DSO and inventory turnover there are what could fairly be called industry norms or industry standards. In most cases there are only modest deviations from those standards.

For the DSO the industry norm is fairly precise as usually there are industry-standard terms of sale. If most firms are at 2%, 10/net 30, it is challenging for a single firm to establish its own differing terms of sale. As a result, most of the deviation with regard to DSO arises from how strict the firm is in adhering to those terms. Some firms enforce collections aggressively while others are much more relaxed.

The inventory turnover differences between firms are much greater. Turnover within a line of trade tends to be influenced by vendor lead times, seasonality, and the breadth of the assortment required to satisfy customer demand. Every firm approaches these factors differently, but there is a tendency to conduct business in a reasonably similar fashion.

The combination of industry norms and the fact that both inventory and accounts receivable are two-edge swords makes the analysis a little trickier than for the other CPVs. Virtually every firm likes faster sales growth. In addition, the vast majority prefer higher gross margins and lower operating expenses. However, with inventory turnover and the DSO, better could be higher or lower depending upon the firm's view of the trade-off between investment levels and sales support.

The Impact of the DSO

The impact of the DSO on both PBT and ROA will be examined using the same two tests as previously. For the first time in this report, though, the first test produces such a dramatic result that the second test appears redundant.

High/Low Test—Once again, this simple test measures whether the companies that collect faster (relative to their peers) produce better profit levels than those firms that collect more slowly.

The answer is essentially no. There is no difference in the PBT for the two groups of firms. The previous sentence does not say there is no real significant difference, it says there is *no* difference. Both the slow-collection and fast-collection firms have the exact same PBT as shown below.

Collection Category	PBT (%)		
	Low Margin/ Low Expenses	**Mid-Range Margin/Expenses**	**High Margin/ High Expenses**
Sample Firms	1.0	2.5	3.5
Slow Collection	1.0	2.5	3.5
Fast Collection	1.0	2.5	3.5

At the same time, there is a modestly higher ROA for firms that collect faster. For slow-collecting firms the ROA is 7.7%. For fast-collecting firms the ROA rises to 8.4%. It is a difference, but one that pales in comparison to the differences observed for the other CPVs.

The lack of a difference regarding PBT is not terribly surprising given the Goldilocks problem discussed before. Some firms think collecting faster (to the extent industry norms allow) is a sound approach; others think collecting slower is more beneficial. With a large sample, both high-profit and low-profit firms fall into each DSO category. The rate of collections simply doesn't change the PBT.

While the lack of a difference for PBT is somewhat understandable, the small variation in ROA is surprising. Reducing accounts receivable (shortening the DSO) should lower the carrying costs. There should be lower interest expense, fewer costs of following up with slow-paying accounts and reduced bad debts. In addition, a reduction in accounts receivable should lower the overall investment in the firm.

Mathematically, reducing accounts receivable increases the numerator in the ROA equation (lower expenses) and decreases the denominator (lower investment). Conceptually, there should be a large ROA delta. Instead there is only a small one. This is not to say that the DSO is entirely irrelevant. It does say that the relationship between the DSO and profitability is much more complicated than for other CPVs.

Continuous Improvement Test—It is still possible that despite the lack of a profound impact from the DSO there are some profit implications as firms vary from industry norms. This seems particularly possible since there is considerable debate as to whether the DSO should be high as a result of using accounts receivable as a sales tool or whether it should be low to provide proper investment control.

The quintiles used in the examination of DSO are:

- **Very Slow**—More than 17.5% slower.
- **Slow**—Between 5.0% and 17.5% slower.
- **Mid-Range**—Between 5.0% slower and 5.0% faster.
- **Fast**—Between 5.0% and 25.0% faster.
- **Very Fast**—More than 25.0% faster.

Once again there is a non-symmetrical distribution. The slowest-collecting group is only 17.5% slower than typical while the fastest group is 25.0% faster. Using 30 days as an illustrative collection period, the very slow collecting firms get paid in 35.3 days while the more aggressive firms collect in 22.5 days.

Exhibit 7 reviews the profit implications associated with the quintiles. It is possible for different people to interpret the exhibit in very different ways. The underlying noise in the sample makes precise identification of differences difficult when they are not as pronounced as they were, for example, with operating expenses. With that caveat in mind, three differences appear important.

First, firms that collect slowly enjoy a somewhat higher PBT but pay an investment penalty that results in a moderately lower ROA. Assuming that the higher PBT comes as a result of higher sales volume and the potential for a higher gross margin, this may well be a legitimate trade-off for some firms.

Second, for firms that collect fast there is almost no PBT advantage, but there is a decided ROA advantage. Taken collectively, these two results suggest that all of the ROA improvement comes from the reduced investment level aspect of the ROA formula.

Third, the firms in the third quintile do worse than anybody else and do so by a rather large margin. This is surprising given the industry norm on collections that was discussed earlier. Just being near the norm apparently triggers a profitability penalty. With credit programs, it may be necessary to be clearly fish or fowl.

Whatever the underlying factors, the ROA implications of the quintiles are decidedly mixed:

Collection Category	ROA (%)
Sample Firms	8.0
Very Slow	7.5
Slow	8.2
Mid-Range	7.0
Fast	8.7
Very Fast	8.9

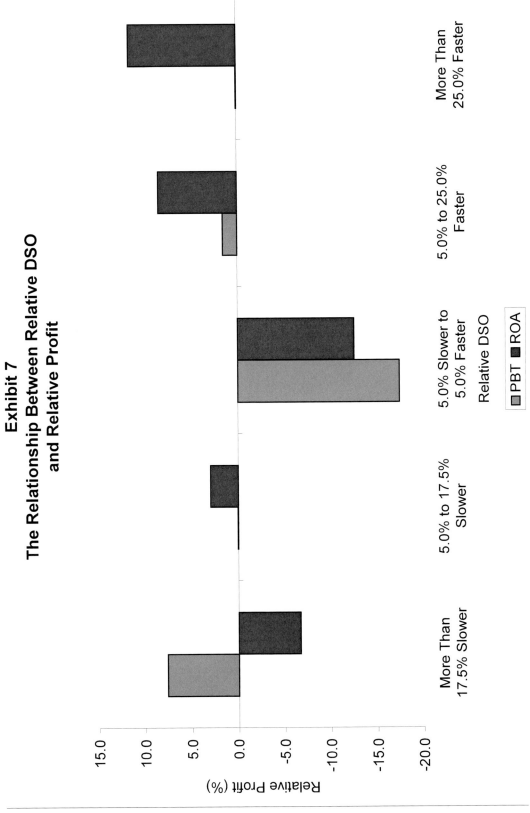

Exhibit 7
The Relationship Between Relative DSO and Relative Profit

Unfortunately, the results suggest what not to do much more than they suggest what to do. The "what not to do" is to avoid being just another firm. The "what to do" depends upon the goals of the firm. A case can be made for collecting slower or collecting faster as long as either tactic is part of a precise operating plan.

The Impact of Inventory Turnover

The examination of the impact of inventory on distributor profitability will once again employ the two tests used previously. As with accounts receivable, the first test produces stark results that reduces the role of the second test to merely trying to provide an explanation.

High/Low Test—The first test measures whether or not companies that generate a higher inventory turnover (relative to their peers) produce better profit levels than those firms that turn their inventory more slowly.

The result is almost identical in structure to that seen for accounts receivable. The firms with a high inventory turnover have the exact same relative PBT as the firms with a low rate of inventory turnover.

Inventory Turnover Category	PBT (%)		
	Low Margin/ Low Expenses	Mid-Range Margin/Expenses	High Margin/ High Expenses
Sample Firms	1.0	2.5	3.5
Low Turnover	1.0	2.5	3.5
High Turnover	1.0	2.5	3.5

At the ROA level there is an important difference. The high-turnover firms (using the 8.0% ROA base) have an ROA of 9.0%. Meanwhile, the low-turn firms have an ROA of 7.4%.

The lack of a PBT difference combined with a fairly significant ROA difference needs to be fully understood. The implication is that the reduction in inventory carrying costs associated with higher turns is offset by some combination of factors deriving from having less inventory. These could be missed sales, lower gross margin or even offsetting expenses associated with having less inventory.

Whatever the underlying reason, a PBT impact simply does not exist. However, the investment reduction is significant. It drives the entire improvement in ROA.

Continuous Improvement Test—The mixed message regarding inventory turnover and profitability can be clarified somewhat by examining the performance quintiles.

The quintiles used in the examination of Inventory Turnover are:

- **Very Low**—More than 30.0% lower.
- **Low**—Between 10.0% and 30.0% lower.
- **Mid-Range**—Between 10.0% lower and 10.0% higher.
- **High**—Between 10.0% and 40.0% higher.
- **Very High**—More than 40.0% higher.

It is worth noting that the percentage variations from typical are much larger for inventory turnover than for the DSO. The industry structural norms regarding credit terms are fairly rigid within a line of trade. The norms with regard to turnover can be ameliorated with management actions.

Exhibit 8 reviews the profit implications associated with the quintiles. Once again, the underlying noise associated with empirical data creates some interpretation problems. However, three tentative conclusions can be drawn.

First, the profit penalty associated with a very-low inventory turnover is huge, whether measured in terms of either ROA or PBT. A very-low turnover probably reflects an inventory investment that is close to out of control. Consequently, there are probably significant carrying costs weighing down the firm. There is also the real potential that if a significant portion of the inventory is dead, then the firm's service level is suffering even in light of a heavy inventory commitment.

Second, the higher turnover firms are something of a mixed bag. Firms doing slightly better than typical actually have lower profit performance. Only at the extreme high end is there a clear ROA advantage. However, PBT is merely typical for the highest-turnover quintile.

Third, the firms in the third quintile do better than everyone else and do so by a rather large margin. It might be remembered that with regard to DSO the middle group did much worse than everybody else. Such somewhat incongruent findings leave researchers grasping for conclusions.

It is very possible that at both ends of the spectrum firms are having service level issues either because of too little inventory in stock or too much dead inventory. Seemingly, firms in the mid-range group avoid this issue. There are other potential reasons that could be offered. All that can be said for now is that typical is actually best.

Regardless of the reasons behind the ROA pattern, it does exist:

Inventory Turnover Category	ROA (%)
Sample Firms	8.0
Very Low	4.8
Low	8.0
Mid-Range	9.9
High	7.6
Very High	9.0

As with accounts receivable, the results provide more direction for what not to do. In particular, it is essential to not fall way below the industry norm with regard to turnover. However, moving well above the industry norm is not necessarily a great idea either. The key seems to be to operate in the middle.

Conclusions Regarding
Accounts Receivable and Inventory

Both the DSO and inventory turnover have a very mixed relationship to profitability, measured in terms of either PBT or ROA. The relationships that do exist impact profit results in very different ways.

For the DSO it appears to be necessary to stake out some position towards one of the extremes. Whether that should be a higher or lower DSO depends upon which measure of profitability is most important to the firm—PBT or ROA. The greatest PBT comes from slower collections, the highest ROA from faster collections.

In sharp contrast it is firms with an inventory turnover close to typical that enjoy the greatest profit potential (both PBT and ROA). The penalty from carrying excessive inventory is particularly significant.

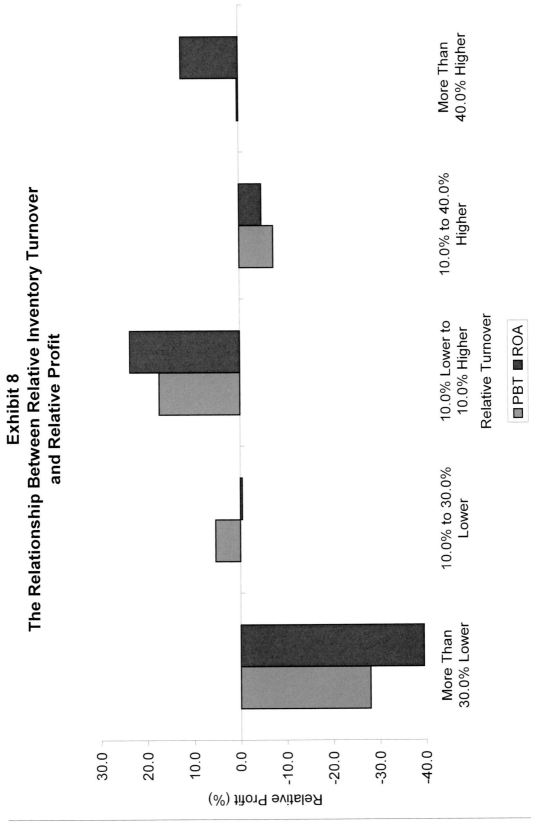

Exhibit 8
The Relationship Between Relative Inventory Turnover
and Relative Profit

■ Section Five:
The Profitability Sweet Spot

The previous sections identified the impact of the CPVs individually. In this section attention will turn to how the CPVs could—or even should—be combined to produce the largest possible profit.

One obvious approach is that the firm should do everything better than its competitors. This is an extension of the High/Low Test that was used in the previous sections. It means that the firm performs better than the typical firm on *each* of the CPVs. That is, it has higher sales volume, more rapid sales growth, a higher gross margin percentage and a lower operating expense percentage than its peers. It also has a higher rate of inventory turnover and collects faster, even though those two CPVs were noted to be double-edge swords.

Doing everything better than the firm's peers is, of course, easier said than done. Actually, it is close to impossible to do. Out of the 885 firms in the research project, exactly 9 had a perfect score on managing all of the CPVs better than the typical firm in their lines of trade. Their reward is a PBT that is 128.6% higher than typical and an ROA that is 182.5% higher.

Even if firms tried to achieve perfection, they are unlikely to reach it. Every firm has a tendency to emphasize some part of the business more than others. Some firms have a sales orientation, others emphasize asset control and the like. This simply reflects the different perspectives of different management teams. Few firms—9 out of 885, or barely more than 1.0%—can reach perfection.

However, it may not be necessary to strive for perfection. It might be possible to identify a group of CPVs that could be managed collectively to produce a strong profit improvement. That effort is the theme of this section.

A Three-Pronged Approach

This section examines the profit results associated with being better than the typical firm on *any three* of the six different CPVs. Again, this harks back to the High/ Low Test that was used throughout the previous three sections. It does not involve being in the fourth or fifth quintile on any of the CPVs. It merely involves being better than the industry norm on three CPVs.

As an illustration, the firm might be above typical in sales size, have a higher gross margin and collect faster. A second scenario might be to have faster sales growth, lower expenses and a higher rate of inventory turnover.

Three out of six is an arbitrary number, of course. It is not suggested that such an approach is ideal or even preferable to other combinations. Companies might very well strive to do better on two out of six or four out of six. It is, however, a relatively common theme in management—do three things better. It is also a group of CPV combinations that can be analyzed within the current data set.

There were six different CPVs evaluated in the previous sections of this report—sales size, sales growth, gross margin percentage, operating expense percentage, the DSO and inventory turnover. Three actions at a time produces twenty different CPV combinations. For want of better terminology, these will be referred to as twenty different Profit Plans.

It is important to remember that for both the DSO and inventory turnover, quicker is viewed as better. There is some debate regarding this, as was noted earlier. However, the prevailing mentality in distribution at the present time is that firms should try to collect faster and have a higher rate of inventory turnover.

The Profit Implications of Different Profit Plans

The first part of this section will examine how the plans impact PBT; the second part will relate the plans to ROA. PBT is being covered first simply because it is the profit ratio that most managers review most frequently.

Exhibit 9 lists all of the plans ranked from the one with the largest positive impact on PBT down to the one with the smallest impact. The left side of the exhibit consists of a series of check marks identifying which of the three CPVs are incorporated into the specific profit plan. For each of the twenty plans three items are reported:

- **Impact on PBT**—The percentage change in the PBT generated by the firms following each particular plan. As was the case throughout the earlier sections, this is based on the deviation from the median PBT.
- **Resulting PBT**—Using the three different sample firms from Exhibit 1 as a baseline, this presents the actual PBTs that would be produced if the statistical relationships held true.
- **Number of Firms**—This totals 1,924 firms which is a little more than twice the number of firms in the research project. This is because some firms fall into more than one category. For example, if a firm does four things well it will be assigned to two distinct three-at-a-time categories. A very few (9 firms) do everything well and some perform under the line-of-trade median on every factor.

Exhibit 9
An Analysis of Twenty Different Profit Plans
and Their Impact on PBT

	Sales Size	Sales Growth	GM	Oper. Exp.	DSO	Inv. Turn	Relative PBT	Low	Mid	High	Number of Firms
1			✓	✓	✓		147.5	2.5	6.2	8.7	42
2	✓		✓	✓			122.2	2.2	5.6	7.8	53
3		✓	✓	✓			120.5	2.2	5.5	7.7	42
4			✓	✓		✓	118.8	2.2	5.5	7.7	37
5		✓	✓	✓	✓		65.6	1.7	4.1	5.8	121
6	✓		✓	✓	✓		60.9	1.6	4.0	5.6	113
7	✓	✓			✓		58.7	1.6	4.0	5.6	104
8	✓		✓			✓	57.9	1.6	3.9	5.5	71
9	✓	✓	✓		✓		57.9	1.6	3.9	5.5	79
10	✓	✓	✓			✓	56.1	1.6	3.9	5.5	96
11				✓	✓	✓	50.0	1.5	3.8	5.3	124
12	✓	✓		✓			46.3	1.5	3.7	5.1	158
13	✓	✓	✓		✓	✓	43.5	1.4	3.6	5.0	97
14		✓	✓		✓	✓	40.6	1.4	3.5	4.9	73
15	✓				✓	✓	36.8	1.4	3.4	4.8	96
16	✓	✓				✓	31.3	1.3	3.3	4.6	119
17	✓	✓		✓	✓	✓	31.0	1.3	3.3	4.6	145
18	✓			✓	✓	✓	28.9	1.3	3.2	4.5	154
19		✓	✓		✓	✓	28.8	1.3	3.2	4.5	114
20	✓	✓	✓		✓	✓	3.4	1.0	2.6	3.6	86
	✓	✓	✓	✓	✓	✓	128.6	2.3	5.7	8.0	9

As can be seen, *every* unique combination of three CPVs, when taken collectively, has a positive impact on PBT. This suggests that if a firm could focus randomly on any three CPVs and perform above the line-of-trade norm on those three, the resulting PBT also would be above the line-of-trade norm.

However, the improvement levels are far from equal. The range of impact is from 147.5% better for Plan One to 3.4% for Plan Twenty. Every combination produces results that are better than typical, but the range of improvement is massive.

Interestingly, managing all six of the CPVs more effectively increased PBT by 128.6% as shown at the bottom of the exhibit. The top four plans were virtually as profitable as the "all six" plan. This *may* reflect the benefit of doing a few things very well as opposed to doing everything fairly well.

The exhibit also indicates that the plans at the top of the list are heavily geared towards gross margin and especially operating expenses. Specifically, all six of the top profit plans involve controlling operating expenses. Four of the six also employ gross margin.

At the other extreme, all seven of the lowest-PBT impact plans included inventory turnover. Sales growth was a component of four of the seven lowest plans. The DSO and sales size were included in three.

Easily the most arresting finding in Exhibit 9 is that the combinations with the greatest impact on PBT are the least likely to be used by firms in the study. In point of fact, the four most-profitable plans were the four with the lowest incidence.

From a frequency of usage or "popularity" perspective, four out of the five most popular profit plans included sales growth as a component. This is consistent with the popularity of sales as an educational topic in distribution that was discussed in Section One.

Exhibit 10 provides a graphical representation of the data that was presented in Exhibit 9. For each of the twenty profit plans, the exhibit graphs the relative impact on PBT on the horizontal axis versus the number of firms employing the plan (incidence) on the vertical axis.

The imbalance between the impact on PBT and usage in distribution is obvious. The four real profit-enhancing combinations are resting somewhat forlornly at the lower right-hand corner of the exhibit.

It is not quite as obvious, but there is a popularity cluster of six plans towards the upper-left side of the graph. All six are widely implemented but are in the bottom half of the plans in terms of PBT improvement. The disconnect between the potential profit impact and the level of usage is disconcerting.

As long as increasing sales is viewed as fun and lowering operating expenses is viewed as drudgery, distributors may continue to emphasize CPV combinations

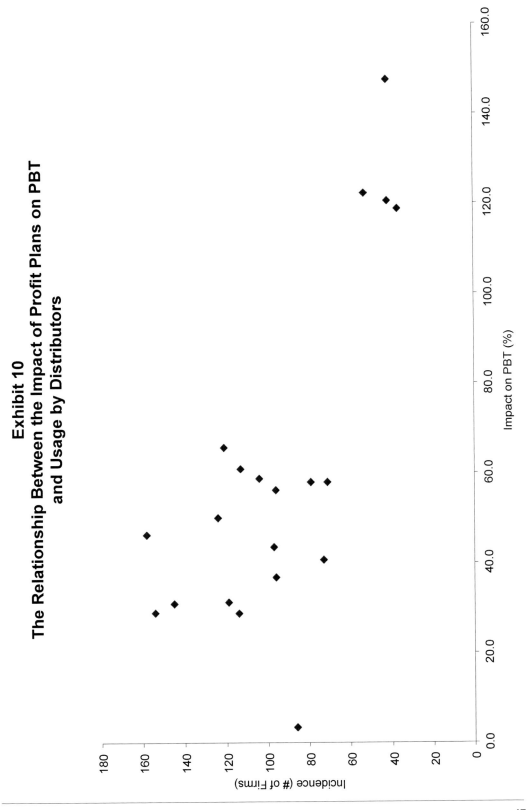

Exhibit 10
The Relationship Between the Impact of Profit Plans on PBT and Usage by Distributors

towards the bottom of the list in Exhibit 9. If increasing PBT can be defined as fun, then there is an opportunity to line up usage—enthusiasm if you will—with profit potential.

Exhibit 11 takes the same exact approach that was employed in Exhibit 9, but applies it to ROA. The list of profit plans in Exhibit 11 is identical to the list that was in Exhibit 9. Since PBT and ROA are highly correlated, there is a very strong degree of similarity between the two exhibits. However, the profit plans are ranked in a slightly different order.

Since ROA incorporates the investment component in measuring performance, both the DSO and inventory turnover rise somewhat in the rankings. This is true at both the top and the bottom of the list. Despite these slight modifications the lists are very similar.

Despite the re-ranking, the top four combinations in Exhibit 9 are also the top four combinations in Exhibit 11, albeit in slightly different order. They also continue, of course, to be the four that are employed the least by the firms in the research project.

It is useful to compare the impact of these four plans with the "all six" plan mentioned earlier. With regard to ROA there is a premium (182.5% higher ROA) from performing above the norm on every CPV. This is because two of the CPVs in the six-pronged plan incorporate a lower level of asset investment.

Exhibit 12 provides a graphical interpretation of Exhibit 11. The structure remains the same as Exhibit 10, but the extremes are moderated somewhat. Even with less polarization, the differences between popularity and performance remain obvious.

The Usage Conundrum

Collectively, the four previous exhibits concluded three things: First, performing better on any combination of three CPVs will improve financial results. Second, there is a wide variation in the profit impact from different CPV combinations. Third, the most popular combinations do not produce the greatest impact on profits.

Exhibit 13 combines these three conclusions. It does so by examining the impact on PBT and ROA on the two axes of the graph. It then incorporates an analysis of the extent to which the different plans are employed.

The exhibit utilizes what is commonly called a bubble graph. The size of the bubble graphically represents the extent to which a particular profit plan is utilized. The larger the bubble, the more popular the plan is. The location of the bubbles reflects the plan's impact on both PBT and ROA.

Bubbles towards the right represent plans with a large impact on ROA. Bubbles towards the top indicate plans with a large impact on PBT. Bubbles towards the upper right are plans with a significant impact on both PBT and ROA.

Exhibit 11
An Analysis of Twenty Different Profit Plans and Their Impact on ROA

	Sales Size	Sales Growth	GM	Oper. Exp.	DSO	Inv. Turn	Relative ROA	Resulting ROA	Number of Firms
1			✓	✓	✓		156.4	20.5	42
2			✓	✓		✓	131.5	18.5	37
3		✓	✓	✓			117.6	17.4	42
4	✓		✓	✓			83.1	14.7	53
5	✓	✓		✓	✓		69.9	13.6	121
6	✓			✓	✓		66.7	13.3	113
7	✓	✓		✓	✓	✓	64.3	13.1	104
8					✓	✓	63.6	13.1	124
9	✓		✓		✓	✓	56.6	12.5	96
10	✓					✓	56.2	12.5	71
11	✓	✓		✓			54.8	12.4	158
12	✓		✓		✓		51.5	12.1	79
13	✓	✓	✓			✓	51.0	12.1	96
14	✓	✓	✓		✓	✓	50.6	12.0	119
15		✓	✓			✓	50.6	12.0	73
16		✓		✓		✓	46.1	11.7	145
17	✓	✓		✓	✓	✓	40.7	11.3	154
18	✓		✓		✓	✓	39.3	11.1	114
19		✓	✓	✓	✓	✓	37.7	11.0	97
20	✓		✓	✓	✓	✓	10.6	8.8	86
							182.5	22.6	9

Four plans clearly are leaders in improving both ROA and PBT. They are, unfortunately, the four CPV combinations that are the least utilized:

- Gross Margin, Operating Expenses and the DSO
- Gross Margin, Operating Expenses and Inventory Turnover
- Gross Margin, Operating Expenses and Sales Growth
- Gross Margin, Operating Expenses and Sales Volume Size

The redundancy of gross margin, operating expenses and something else is obvious. It would appear that the path to increasing profit, at lest empirically, goes through the internal operations aspects of managing margins and expenses.

There is a mass of profit plans that impact both ROA and PBT in a modest way and are widely employed. They are all moderately effective as profit plans, but their profit impact doesn't really justify their prevelance.

Finally, there is one plan that has almost no impact on profitability, but is utilized more extensively than it would seemingly deserve. The plan incorporates gross margin which is part of the four most effective plans. In this case it is combined with an emphasis on both inventory turnover and the DSO.

The amalgam of gross margin and two investment factors as the lowest-performing, but widely-employed profit plan, may be nothing more than a statistical fluke. However, it conjures up memories of outmoded management metrics such as GMROI which try to tie gross margin and inventory (and in some cases gross margin and the DSO) together in a return on investment format.

The use of measures such as GMROI to evaluate items or gross margin per dollar of accounts receivable to evaluate customers continues to doom firms to employing anachronistic concepts in a technological age. More importantly it appears to lead directly to lower profit performance.[4]

Gross Margin and Operating Expenses as the Central Elements of a Profit Plan

Both Exhibits 9 and 11 suggest that the most successful firms combine a strong gross margin percentage with a strong operating expense percentage. After that, it doesn't appear to make any real difference what additional strategy is employed. The problem in improving profitability is that very few firms appear to be able put together any of the most-profitable combinations of CPVs.

The central reason behind this is that gross margin percentage and the operating expense percentage are the only two independent variables in the analysis that are highly correlated. That means, quite simply, that firms with a high gross margin percentage almost always have a high operating expense percentage as well.

---

4   For a discussion of the problems with GMROI and suggestions for new approaches, see *Saying Goodbye to GMROI*, profitplanninggroup.com. The white paper is in the Seminars section.

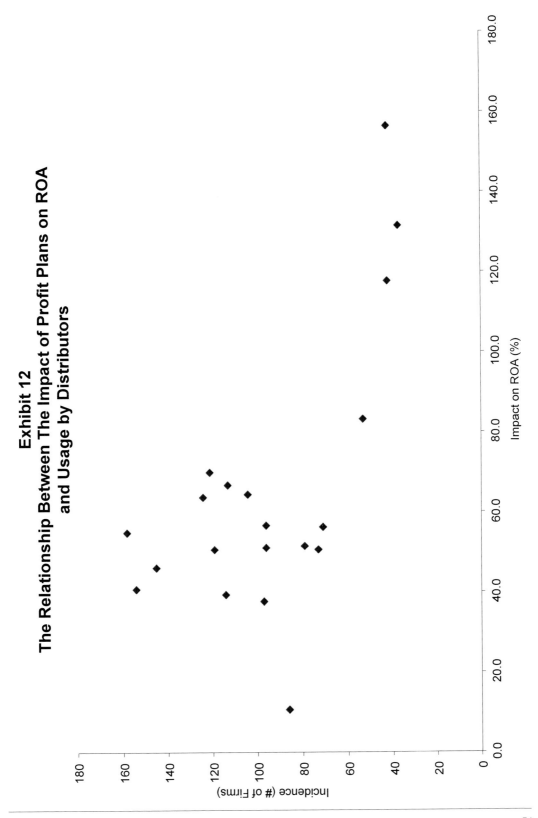

Exhibit 12
The Relationship Between The Impact of Profit Plans on ROA and Usage by Distributors

Raising the gross margin percentage relative to operating expenses is challenging. Combining a high gross margin percentage with a low operating expense percentage moves from challenging to incredibly difficult.

However, it seems likely that any firm able to modify or break the gross margin/ operating expense relationship should generate exceptional profits. Consequently, it is useful to take a more detailed look at various gross margin and operating expenses relationships.

Specifically, this analysis looks at those firms that are able to move beyond the mid-point with regard to *both* gross margin and operating expenses and into at least the fourth quintile. This means that the firms are not performing inordinately well on either variable. By definition, they are merely better than 60.0% of the firms in the research project. What sets them apart was that they were able to outperform 60.0% of the firms on both metrics at the same time.

Only 35 out of 885 firms—slightly less than 4.0%—are able to reach this level of performance. However, the reward for doing so is huge. This group of firms collectively produces an ROA that is 189.7% higher than the norm. Put into actual ROA terms, they have a 15.2% ROA versus the 8.0% base results.

Given that both gross margin and operating expenses impact PBT and do not impact asset investments, the PBT difference is even greater. Firms in the superior group have a PBT that is 226.3% higher than the norm.

Any standard that can only be reached by 4.0% of the firms probably continues to be overly-aggressive in character. In an attempt to find a somewhat more attainable set of targets, three less-stringent performance combinations were examined.

- **Good Gross Margin/Adequate Operating Expenses**—This combination includes the firms that are in the top two quintiles with regard to gross margin (top 40.0% of the firms) and whose operating expenses were at least better than the typical firm. It can be thought of as a 40.0%/50.0% model.
- **Adequate Gross Margin/Good Operating Expenses**—This is simply the mirror image of the previous plan. It includes firms whose gross margin is at least better than the typical firm and is in the top two quintiles in controlling operating expenses. This is a 50.0%/40.0% model.
- **Good Gross Margin and Operating Expenses**—This raises the performance bar slightly by requiring results in the top two quintiles on both factors. This is characterized here as the 40.0%/40.0% model. This is the scenario that was discussed at the beginning of this section.

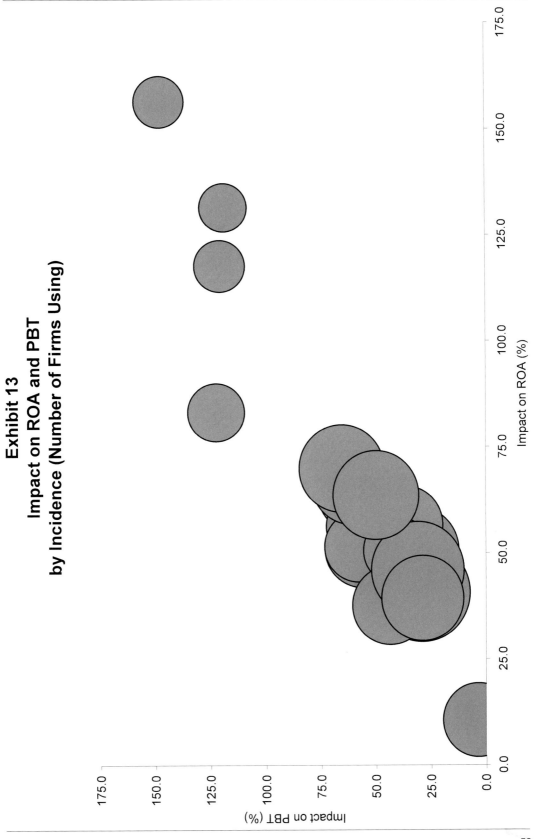

Exhibit 13
Impact on ROA and PBT
by Incidence (Number of Firms Using)

Impact on ROA (%)

Impact on PBT (%)

The profit results for any set of firms with superior performance with regard to both gross margin and operating expenses is impressive. The following table summarizes the results of the three combinations:

Gross Margin	Oper. Exp.	Improvement In	
		PBT (%)	ROA(%)
Top 40%	Top 50%	163.5	128.6
Top 50%	Top 40%	154.7	151.5
Top 40%	Top 40%	226.3	189.7

The profit improvements overwhelmingly demonstrate the importance of generating better than typical performance on both the gross margin percentage and the operating expense percentage. The clear implication is that firms need to know with some precision their position in their industry with regard to both factors. After that, they need to develop programs to reach the top 40% on at least one of the factors. Subsequent to those actions, it is somewhat immaterial what additional profit variables are emphasized.

Conclusions About the CPVs

Research projects can do no more than provide insights into the operating dynamics of distributors. Ultimately, management must make the decision whether the research points towards a path that the firm can follow. This research clearly suggests that cost control via operational excellence has the greatest likelihood to improve profitability. If a firm has no appetite for controlling costs, then significant profit improvement will prove elusive.

Having said that, the four top profit-generating plans all combine gross margin and operating expenses. This combination can only be ignored if the firm can achieve top quintile performance, or better, on all of the other CPVs. It is difficult to imagine a reason why any firm would try to optimize performance on secondary CPVs when reasonable performance on gross margin and operating expenses holds such significant profit potential.

Interestingly if there is a stampede towards combining gross margin and operating expenses into a profit plan, the potential impact of such a plan may be reduced by overuse. That appears to be a risk worth taking.

■ Section Six:
Implications for Action

It is one thing to understand what drives profitability in distribution; it is something else entirely to turn that understanding into action. Converting the research findings into a viable plan requires three separate, distinct steps. The first is dependent upon joint activity by an amalgam of like-minded firms. The last two necessitate individual initiative by firms interested in real profit improvement. The three steps must be sequenced:

- **Benchmarking Participation**—First, firms must take part in a benchmarking effort through a trade association or buying group in order to have the information set necessary to support action.
- **Integrated Financial Planning**—Second, the firm must incorporate the benchmarking results into the financial planning process of the firm. This necessitates tying the firm's actions back to the results of the benchmarking project.
- **Total Firm Commitment**—Finally, the firm must ensure that all stakeholders know where the firm is going and how it is to get there. This is a unilateral action that must be taken by each individual firm.

Benchmarking Participation: Supporting an Essential Group Activity

Everything in this report is based upon precise benchmarking information. Without such data as a baseline, there is no basis for improvement. Therefore, the essential first step in improving profitability is to take part in a sound benchmarking program.

Most benchmarking programs in distribution are supported by trade associations. In point of fact, all 17 lines of trade included in this report were sponsored by a trade association. Absent trade association support, some benchmarking efforts are backed by buying groups. A very few such programs are authorized by suppliers who are actively interested in the strength of their distributor channel partners.

Regardless of sponsorship, benchmarking programs must meet two criteria. First, they must provide adequate information on the CPVs and the factors that support those CPVs. Second, they must represent an adequate sample of the line of trade.

Many of the current benchmarking efforts in distribution are outstanding in terms of both the depth of information provided and the participation rate of the members. Most are at least adequate with regard to both factors. However, a few are deficient on either one or both of the requirements.

With information depth and adequate participation it is possible to provide participants with the sort of analytical support shown in **Exhibit 14**. The key item to note in the exhibit is that for each of the performance ratios, the firm's performance has been put into percentile mode. This allows management to think in terms of the quintiles that were used throughout this report.

However, benchmarking reports aren't designed around the results of this research project with the data organized into quintiles. The reports are designed around the needs of the group supporting the benchmarking project. In the case of Exhibit 14, quartiles are used instead of quintiles. Other benchmarking reports build the comparative structure on percentiles.

No matter what methodology is used, what is important is to be able to clearly identify where the firm stands relative to its peers. Without the relative standards, the information is not actionable.

On the very top line, the firm has a PBT of 3.0% which puts it into the 55th percentile. The bar associated with that variable goes out 55.0% of the way to the far right. Management has a clear and unambiguous understanding of where it stands versus the industry.

One of the ways the firm earned the somewhat higher PBT is through a strong gross margin percentage. That can be seen on the seventh line item. The firm's gross margin is 25.0% which, for this line of trade, puts it somewhere around the top 40.0% of the firms.

Such specific comparisons are essential to making benchmarking results a true profit-improvement tool. It is not good enough for the firm to have a vague idea that it is "above average" or is "doing good" in terms of performance. Improvement on the critical profit variables requires knowing precisely where the firm stands in order to know how much of an improvement is needed.

A second important issue highlighted by the exhibit is that there is sufficient supporting detail behind each of the CPVs. For example, with regard to gross margin, there is data on the gross margin generated by warehouse (stock) sales, special orders and drop shipments. These are in the section labeled gross margin.

Exhibit 14
Participant Scorecard

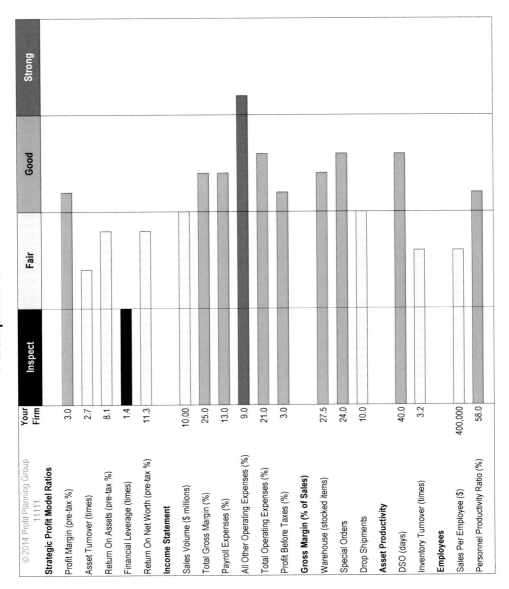

	Your Firm	Inspect	Fair	Good	Strong
Strategic Profit Model Ratios					
Profit Margin (pre-tax %)	3.0				
Asset Turnover (times)	2.7				
Return On Assets (pre-tax %)	8.1				
Financial Leverage (times)	1.4				
Return On Net Worth (pre-tax %)	11.3				
Income Statement					
Sales Volume ($ millions)	10.00				
Total Gross Margin (%)	25.0				
Payroll Expenses (%)	13.0				
All Other Operating Expenses (%)	9.0				
Total Operating Expenses (%)	21.0				
Profit Before Taxes (%)	3.0				
Gross Margin (% of Sales)					
Warehouse (stocked items)	27.5				
Special Orders	24.0				
Drop Shipments	10.0				
Asset Productivity					
DSO (days)	40.0				
Inventory Turnover (times)	3.2				
Employees					
Sales Per Employee ($)	400,000				
Personnel Productivity Ratio (%)	58.0				

Barriers to Benchmarking

Despite the value of benchmarking, probably fewer than one percent of all distributors actively engage in benchmarking their financial results in a meaningful way. There are two factors behind this abysmally low number—the lack of a relevant benchmarking group and the lack of participation when benchmarking opportunities do exist.

Benchmarking Group—Fewer than half of all affiliated trade association members of the NAW (the premier group of trade associations in distribution) provide benchmarking services to their members. In many cases, buying groups have filled this void. However, for too many firms there is simply no way to benchmark. Every idea about performance on the CPVs is anecdotal rather than empirical.

Participation Level—Even among associations that do provide a benchmarking service, participation is often discouragingly low. Typically, only around 15.0% of the members of any distributor association participate in the benchmarking program. There are numerous reasons for lack of participation, but most of them are related to an inability to understand the value of the service or concerns about data security.

The result is that even where benchmarking is an active, on-going process, somewhere around 85% of the firms have no real basis for making improvements in performance. They are trying to navigate an ever-changing world without a road map.

Finally, as was noted earlier, even when financial benchmarking services are provided, the quality of such efforts varies widely. Some programs are one-off activities that do not maintain the statistical rigor necessary for reporting meaningful results. Even well-designed benchmarking programs often fail to provide the detail on *percentile performance* that was highlighted in Exhibit 14.

Integrated Financial Planning:
The Linkage Between Information and Action

Once the firm has determined its percentile position on the CPVs (gross margin, expenses, etc.) and resulting profitability variables (ROA and PBT) it must then develop an improvement plan. Seemingly, this should be a simple process. The firm merely maps out the steps required to improve results and then implements the plan as aggressively as possible. Frequently, this simple process goes awry.

There are two related problems that stand between the firm and a meaningful profit plan. The first is the inability to understand exactly how improvements in performance will change the firm's percentile ranking. That is, there is no interactive linkage back to the benchmarking results for the firm.

The second problem derives directly from the lack of the interactive linkage. In its absence firms tend to overplan. That is, they set goals that are simply unobtainable. Ultimately, unobtainable becomes dysfunctional.

Interactive Linkage

Virtually very firm employs some sort of financial model which can evaluate changes in performance. That is, they operate in a "what if" mode, typically using programs such as Excel, to see how increased sales or gross margin impacts overall results. The problem is that the "what ifs" are merely changes that are not based on a benchmarking process as outlined above.

What is needed is some sort of planning system that ties the performance plan directly to the firm's various percentile rankings in the benchmarking program. That is, the planning system should be able to provide feedback as to how changes in a CPV cause the firm's percentile performance to change.

This is a somewhat complicated process, but can be achieved fairly readily if the firm's planning process is linked to the benchmarking system. In practice this linkage is greatly facilitated by some sort of interactive Financial Dashboard that is a structural component of the benchmarking project.

The way that such a dynamic financial dashboard can impact financial planning is shown in **Exhibits 15 and 16**. As a starting point, it should be noted that the dashboard uses the green, yellow, red designation most common in such dashboards. At the far right the dashboard also supplies a "check" function to see greater detail regarding each dashboard item.

On the first line of Exhibit 15, the company's current ROA is only 6.3%. This puts it in the 38th percentile. Referring back to the quintile analysis concept used throughout the report, the firm is toward the top of the second quintile. It is far from an ideal position. The firm's PBT position is almost exactly the same, in the 37th percentile.

Dropping down to the third and fourth lines, it can be seen that the firm has a sub-par gross margin percentage and a strong operating expense percentage. This is one more example of gross margin and operating expenses being linked. The profit challenge is to unlink them.

Two more factors also pop up on the dashboard. The firm's asset turnover is low, which helps contribute to the low return on assets. Offsetting this, the firm has a sales growth rate of 17.6%, which is strong enough to put it into the 85th percentile in its line of trade. All of these factors combine to produce a rapidly-growing company facing a serious profit headwind.

The limitation so far is that the firm is only looking over its shoulder. There is the issue of what to do to generate real profit improvements. One philosophy might be to build on the firm's strong operating expense percentage. This involves identifying where the firm has advantages versus the industry and using them as a competitive weapon. Such an approach would point toward sales growth.

A second, and more widely used, philosophy is to attack the areas where there is the largest shortfall compared to industry peers. That leads directly to the gross margin percentage and the desire to maintain its mid-range performance on operating expenses.

Exhibit 16 demonstrates the value of a dynamic dashboard. In this instance, the firm has established a potential plan to moderate its sales growth. The plan calls for increasing the number of invoice lines by 6.0%.

At the same time, the firm plans to increase its prices by 1.5% which will drive its gross margin to 21.2% and put it into the 46th percentile. It will also lead to an increase in sales deriving from the higher prices. Finally, payroll expenses are planned to increase by 3.0% and all other operating expenses by 5.0%.

The overall result is that ROA and profit margin both increase. ROA moves to the 59th percentile while profit margin moves to the 68th. Important improvements have been made. The improvements were accomplished with only small changes in the selected CPVs.

No dashboard can specify how the increase will be achieved. That is part of the management plan supporting the changes on the dashboard. What the dashboard can do is illustrate the changes in relative performance that accompany the management actions.

The benefit of an industry-specific dynamic dashboard is that the firm is always measuring its potential against the industry. It is not just making isolated, somewhat arbitrary changes. The result is a much more meaningful financial plan. It avoids the issue of overplanning.

Overplanning

It is wonderful when firms plan. It is something less than wonderful when firms plan the wrong way. Without something akin to a dynamic financial dashboard outlined above there is a real tendency to plan the wrong way. Every management team is susceptible to overplanning.

Absent industry-specific comparisons, firms tend to produce plans that are overly-aggressive with regard to changes in the CPVs. The plans are not developed wildly, they are simply developed blindly. The result is a chronic case of overplanning.[5]

In a classic over-planning scenario the firm develops a highly-aggressive profit im-

---

5   The idea that a firm could actually overplan is somewhat controversial. For an in-depth discussion of the concept, see Dr. Albert D. Bates, *Breaking Down the Profit Barriers in Distribution*, D. M. Kreg Publishing, 2014.

Exhibit 15
A Sample Performance Dashboard: Reported Results

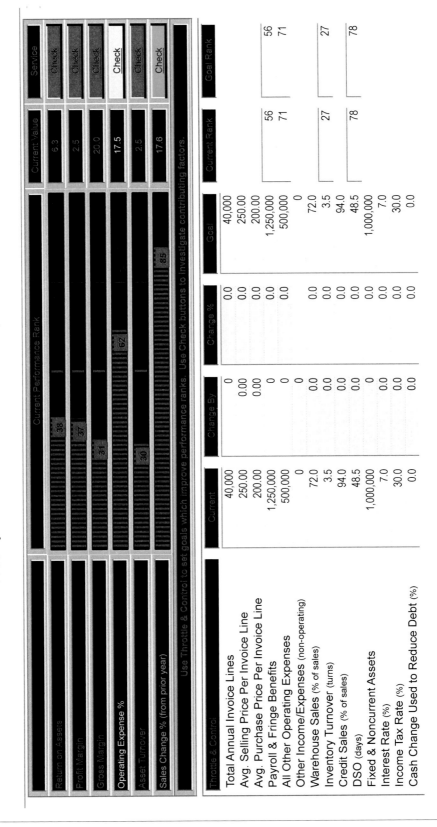

provement plan based upon goals which, in aggregate, are probably unobtainable. Inevitably, the firm falls short of those unreachable aggregate goals. To compensate, the firm sets another round of aggressive goals for the following year. Again, these are not met. Ultimately, the firm develops a behavior pattern of not meeting its goals. To a certain extent it has moved into a "why bother" mode of planning.

An interactive, dynamic planning model can help firms set realistic, achievable goals. Such percentile-based plans have the potential to allow every firm to enhance its profitability, albeit slowly.

Total Firm Commitment:
A Unilateral Action

Most members of top management have a good idea of where they want the firm to go. That idea may be well developed based upon a realistic profit plan or it may be entirely pie in the sky. Regardless of the quality of the plan, top management knows where it wants to go. Top management also has a fairly strong understanding of financial issues based upon reviewing and discussing the "what if" models mentioned earlier.

In a typical distribution organization, for example one with $10.0 million in revenue as was outlined in Exhibit 1, only about 5.0% or so of the total employee base is in top management. That leaves 95.0% of the employees on the outside of the "where we want to go" awareness group. They are also outside of the financial understanding group.

Of course, many of the other employees do not ever make decisions that could help improve profitability in a meaningful way. This group includes most operating employees such as warehouse workers, truck drivers and clerical employees. These constitute about half of the total head count of employees.

After subtracting this group, there is a large and extremely important core of employees that make decisions impacting profit for the firm in a meaningful way. This includes salespeople (both inside and out), credit and collection staff, pricing specialists, inventory control employees and a wide range of others.

These individuals frequently make important decisions. Without an understanding of basic financial issues, their decisions are made based upon anecdotal information about what drives profit, pure intuition or "what we have always done." Such decisions are seldom profit enhancing.

For example, suppose the firm has the heroic set of goals to increase sales by 10.0% and simultaneously add 1.0 percentage point to gross margin. These are understandable until a decision arises that puts them in conflict. Suppose there is the chance to expand the product offering from a specific supplier. It represents an opportunity to increase sales, but perhaps the gross margin is actually lower than

Exhibit 16

A Sample Performance Dashboard: Changes Made

	Goal Performance Rank	Goal Value	Service
Return on Assets	59	10.9	Check
Profit Margin	46	4.2	Check
Gross Margin	68	21.2	Check
Operating Expense %	68	16.8	Check
Asset Turnover	34	2.6	Check
Sales Change %	51	7.6	Check

Use Throttle & Control to set goals which improve performance ranks. Use Check buttons to investigate contributing factors.

Throttle & Control	Current	Change By	Change %	Goal	Current Rank	Goal Rank
Total Annual Invoice Lines	40,000	2,400	6.0	42,400		
Avg. Selling Price Per Invoice Line	250.00	3.75	1.5	253.75		
Avg. Purchase Price Per Invoice Line	200.00	0.00	0.0	200.00		
Payroll & Fringe Benefits	1,250,000	37,500	3.0	1,287,500	56	64
All Other Operating Expenses	500,000	25,000	5.0	525,000	71	73
Other Income/Expenses (non-operating)	0	0	0.0	0		
Warehouse Sales (% of sales)	72.0	0.0	0.0	72.0		
Inventory Turnover (turns)	3.5	0.0	0.0	3.5	27	27
Credit Sales (% of sales)	94.0	0.0	0.0	94.0		
DSO (days)	48.5	0.0	0.0	48.5	78	78
Fixed & Noncurrent Assets	1,000,000	0	0.0	1,000,000		
Interest Rate (%)	7.0	0.0	0.0	7.0		
Income Tax Rate (%)	30.0	0.0	0.0	30.0		
Cash Change Used to Reduce Debt (%)	0.0	0.0	0.0	0.0		

the firm's current margin.

How employees deal with such issues, which are myriad, is a critical issue. Simply put, if decision-making employees are going to help increase profit, they must have an understanding of the reality of the profit structure of the firm.

Trying to provide every employee with a *detailed* understanding of financial issues would be folly. Very few individuals want to be (or should be) accountants or financial officers. However *every* decision-making employee must understand the basics of profitability.

Most trade associations offer programs in this arena. However, any impartial review of their contents must conclude that they are extremely rudimental. They often cover such issues as how to calculate gross margin, which are important, but very limited in scope. By and large this training does not provide the level of financial understanding required.

Historically, providing more-sophisticated instruction in the field was incredibly time-consuming and expensive. It might involve on-site programs led by a financial consultant or the development of expensive, and completely static, video programs. The benefits were large, but the investment was often prohibitive.

Thanks to changing technology, it is possible to provide targeted and dynamic training to decision-making employees at very low costs. Programs can be developed for individual lines of trade or for specific companies quickly and easily. Such programs can be modified at almost no cost as economic and competitive situations change.

Firms now utilizing such programs have greatly improved the quality of decision making throughout the organization. Every employee is now thinking about moving the company forward in the same direction.

Moving Forward

If distributors are going to improve their profitability in a meaningful way, there are three issues that need to be addressed:

Percentile Benchmarking—Knowing exactly where the firm stands relative to its peers with regard to profit results, such as ROA and PBT, and where it stands on each of the critical profit variables. Just knowing "good" or "bad" is not enough. Detailed percentile results are required.

Benchmarking cannot be episodic. Firms need to have historical results to see how changes have manifested themselves over time. At some point, though, the benchmarking process may appear to be a repetitive, redundant process. It is not.

The ability to see changes over time is essential. The firm must know if it has moved up the profitability ladder over the last five years. If it has not, it needs to know why and what can be done about it.

Realistic Profit-Improvement Planning—The firm must develop meaningful plans that provide the basis for moving up that profit ladder. They must focus on the areas where there is the greatest potential for improvement. The plans also must revolve around achievable, attainable, and realistic goals.

Whole Firm Commitment—Every decision-making employee must understand the basic economics of the firm. They have to know what sort of actions improve performance and what sort degrade it. Only then can the entire firm have a sense of direction for improvement.

Enhancing profitability in distribution will never be an easy undertaking. However, firms that know where they stand, where they want to go and have every employee helping them get there will have a marked advantage in the profitability battle.

■ Appendix

There are a few statistical issues that would interest analysts. Four topics are covered here:

- **Sample**—The size and composition of the sample.
- **Relative Measures**—A discussion of the legitimacy of using relative measures for the independent variables.
- **Definitions**—An explanation of some of the terms used in the report.
- **Correlation Matrix**—A presentation of the correlation coefficients between all of the dependent and independent variables used in the report.

Sample

The sample consists of 885 firms that participate in the financial benchmarking surveys conducted by the Profit Planning Group in distribution. All of the information is obtained via benchmarking projects conducted for trade associations. Because of confidentiality issues the associations are not identified, however, all of the associations are members of the National Association of Wholesaler-Distributors. They are all associations that most distribution experts would recognize immediately.

Associations were excluded from the analysis if they do not conduct a detailed financial benchmarking survey. That is, if they use a highly-truncated income statement in their analysis or do not request a full set of operating metrics in conjunction with the financial information.

Individual firms were excluded only if they did not complete the entire data entry form as part of their association's survey process. These exclusions represented less than 1.0% of the total sample.

Some associations are large, and so are represented by a large number of members in the sample. Other associations are small, so their contribution to the sample is modest. No one association represented more than 15.0% of the total sample.

All of the information is for 2013. This represents a relatively typical year in terms of growth. It is also fairly typical in terms of profit performance. That is, it was not a spectacularly profitable year or an unusually low profit year.

To use a statistical term, the sample is a convenience sample. It is drawn only from associations for which the Profit Planning Group conducts a financial benchmarking survey. It is not a random sample of all distributors operating in the United States.

Even though it is not a random sample, say across 50 different lines of trade, the results can be used without hesitation in thinking about distributor profitability in general. The sample size is large, 885 firms, and the representation is across 17 different lines of trade. It is as comprehensive a sample as is available in distribution today.

Relative Measures

Relative measures are used for all of the independent variables (the CPVs) in this report. This means that the CPVs are *not* analyzed on an absolute basis, but are analyzed *relative* to their peers in the *same line of trade*. As noted in the text, a firm with an 11.0% gross margin in an industry where the norm is 10.0% is doing 10.0% better than the typical firm. At the same time, a firm with a 22.0% gross margin in an industry with a 20.0% norm is also doing 10.0% better.

Relative measures are not used because they are perfect, they are used because they are the best-available of the three alternatives that could be used. It is very important to understand why that is true.

Alternative Approaches Not Employed

Absolute Values—The use of absolute values, such as the actual gross margin or inventory turnover, leads to a high degree of confusion. The wide variation between lines of trade means that any analysis of inventory turnover would simply compare one line of trade to another. It says nothing about the ability to perform better than peers within a line of trade.

Absolute Variations—An alternative to absolute values is to use absolute variations. That is, a company with an 11.0% gross margin in an industry with a 10.0% standard would be assigned a value of +1.0 percentage point. This approach is not without merit.

However, producing a gross margin percentage of 11.0% in a line of trade with a 10.0% standards represents much better performance than producing a 21.0% gross margin in a line of trade with a 20.0% standard. Using absolute variations simply does not pick up the level of significance associated with the higher level of performance.

Therefore, the relative measures became the obvious choice. Relative measures are more difficult to interpret, but lead to much more precise conclusions.

Definitions

Data-driven projects must, by definition, employ some arcane terminology in the analysis. The two most important concepts for this project are reviewed below. They are discussed at their most basic level. Readers desiring a more detailed definition should consult any of the myriad statistics books currently in print or review any of the numerous statistical Web sites available.

Typical—This term is used throughout the report to reflect the performance of a typical firm in each individual line of trade. In all instances typical refers to the median of the data set being analyzed.

The median figure is the one exactly in the middle. That is, half of the firms in a line of trade will perform above the median and half will perform below. For example, if an industry has a median gross margin percentage of 20.0%, then half of the firms will have a gross margin that is below the 20.0% number and half will have a gross margin above it.

Medians are used instead of arithmetic means (averages) as they remove much of the distortion associated with averages. If there are severe outliers in a data set, the average will be influenced by their results. Medians treat outliers as just one more data point and are largely unaffected by them.

Correlation Coefficient—This measures the certainty that an increase in one variable will always coincide with an increase (or possibly decrease) in a second one. The classic example used to explain this involves the relationship between height and weight. Taller people, of course, tend to weigh more than shorter people. However, the relationship is not perfect as some short people are heavy and some tall people are light.

The correlation coefficient (called r in the statistical world) varies from -1 to +1. Using results from the report, a value of +1 for the relationship between the gross margin percentage and PBT would mean that every time the gross margin percentage goes up, PBT goes up as well. A value of -1 would mean that every time the gross margin percentage goes up, PBT goes down.

A value of zero means that there is no relationship at all between two variables. When the gross margin percentage goes up, the PBT might go up, go down or stay the same. A result of zero does not mean there is no relationship between two variables. There may, in fact, be a very complex relationship between the two. It is just not as simple as being assured that the two variables go up or down together.

Correlation Matrix

At various places in the report the discussion involves the correlation between various CPVs and either PBT or ROA. It is useful to understand all of the correlation coefficients between all of the variables. They are presented in the following matrix:

Correlation Coefficient Matrix for
All Independent and Dependent Variables

Variable	Sales Size	Sales Growth	Gross Margin	Oper. Exp.	Inv. Turn	DSO	PBT	ROA
Sales Size	***	0.0206	-0.1413	-0.1761	-0.0199	-0.0020	0.0579	0.0342
Sales Growth		***	-0.0423	-0.0375	-0.0173	0.0362	-0.0002	0.0080
Gross Margin			***	0.8525	-0.0934	-0.0354	0.1021	0.0592
Operating Expenses				***	-0.0897	-0.0134	-0.3278	-0.3394
Inventory Turnover					***	0.0394	0.0370	0.0865
DSO						***	-0.0273	-0.0832
PBT							***	0.8921
ROA								***

About the Author

Dr. Albert D. Bates is founder and Chairman of the Profit Planning Group, the leading provider of financial benchmarking services in distribution. This report is based on the firm's benchmarking research in 17 lines of trade.

He specializes in making financial concepts understandable. In that regard, he makes approximately 50 presentations each year on topics such as Improving the Bottom Line, Getting Serious About Profit, Doing More with Less, and Pricing for Profit. He also writes the quarterly Profit Improvement Reports for distribution trade associations.

He has written extensively in both the professional and trade press, including the *Harvard Business Review,* and *the California Management Review*. In addition he has written numerous books, including *Profit Myths, Triple Your Profit!* and *Breaking Down the Profit Barriers in Distribution*.

Al received his undergraduate degree from the University of Texas at Arlington and his MBA and doctorate from Indiana University. While at Indiana he was one of the first recipients of the Ford Foundation Fellowships in Business Education.

His wife, Rebecca, writes mystery novels under the name Sue Star and women's fiction, urban fantasy and science fiction under a range of *noms de plume*. He has three grown daughters. All four of the charming ladies in his life have black belts in Tae Kwon Do.

Al lives in Boulder, Colorado. Consequently, he is a de rigueur hiking and bicycling enthusiast. He can be contacted via email at bigal6212@gmail.com. He does not now have and never will have a Twitter or Facebook account.

Made in the USA
Middletown, DE
10 March 2015